PRESS *ON!*

PRESS *ON!* YOU CAN

DAVE BARBA

www.ipresson.com

Library of Congress Cataloging-in-Publication Data

Barba, Dave, 1950-
Press on! / Dave Barba.
p. cm.
Summary: "A book to encourage pastors not to give up in the ministry"—Provided by publisher.
ISBN 978-0-9914576-2-5 (perfect bound pbk. : alk. paper)
1. Pastoral theology. 2. Encouragement—Religious aspects—Christianity. I. Title.
BV4011.3.B365 2010
248.8′92—dc22

2010017342

Cover Photo Credit: Dave Barba

The fact that materials produced by other publishers may be referred to in this volume does not constitute an endorsement of the content or theological position of materials produced by such publishers.

All Scripture is quoted from the Authorized King James Version unless otherwise noted.

Press On!
Dave Barba, DSMin

Design by Aaron Dickey
Page layout by Nathan Hutcheon

© 2015 by Press On! Ministries
www.ipresson.com

Printed in the United States of America
All rights reserved

ISBN 978-0-9914576-2-5

15 14 13 12 11 10 9 8 7 6 5 4 3 2 1

To Claudia, who helps me survive

CONTENTS

INTRODUCTION

All over Wisconsin you will find quaint buildings that were once churches but are now libraries, town halls, antique stores, or homes. Closed for various reasons, they represent pastors who started well but were unable to press on. Wisconsin has been called "the graveyard of preachers" because of so many churches that have shut down over the years, "burying" pastors who then quit the ministry.

In 1974, God called my wife, Claudia, and me to plant a new church in Menomonee Falls, Wisconsin, a suburb of Milwaukee. We served there for twelve wonderful years as God built that church. In those years we learned that the ministry could be both wonderful and horrible at the same time. We might be shouting for joy over a spiritual victory while simultaneously weeping because someone had stumbled into sin, disappointed us, or opposed our ministry. That is normal for ministry.

Full-time ministry, like the Christian life, is supernatural warfare. It is a battle (1 Tim. 1:18). The apostle Paul told Timothy to "endure hardness, as a good soldier of Jesus Christ" (2 Tim. 2:3) and to set that example as he went through trials. Praise God for the determination of Paul! He said in Philippians 3:12, "Not as though I had already attained, either were already perfect: but I follow after, if that I may apprehend that for which also I am apprehended of Christ Jesus." The Greek word for "follow after," *dioko*, means to ensue, to press forward, or . . . to press on! Paul never considered himself to have arrived in ministry. He was always ready to learn more, to become more for God. He was determined to press on to be all that God wanted him to be.

Are you tired of spiritual battles? Satan doesn't give you a break, does he? He is always ready, ever anxious, to tempt, discourage, and disarm you. He hates every servant of God and is ready to rejoice if you turn aside from God's calling for your life. Paul was determined to defeat Satan by pressing on. He longed to glorify God, to be all that God created and called him to be. Determination in the battle is what this book is about. In the following pages I will share principles that God has taught me through His Word and life experience. I will share some personal anecdotes and some experiences of others—all related to surviving, and enjoying, the ministry.

I am writing to anyone in full-time ministry—pastors, evangelists, missionaries, and other servant heroes. Since my life experience includes starting churches and assisting many church planters, I will address some of the unique challenges and trials of church planters. Claudia will speak to ministry wives in the final chapter. She has found that the needs of ministry wives are more numerous and complex than most imagine. Obviously, God wants all His children to press on in His will. Therefore, though I have full-time servants in mind, you will find these principles to be keys to victory for all Christians.

In forty years of full-time ministry as a pastor, evangelist, and church planter, I have been tempted to quit a number of times. The truths in this book have been, and continue to be, used of God to help me to press on. I am praying that God will use the following pages to encourage you, to challenge you, to help you to press on. Satan wants you to quit. God wants you to survive. With God's help, you can press on—and enjoy the adventure!

PRESS *ON!* . . . YOU CAN

1

Man can live about forty days without food, about three days without water, about eight minutes without air, but only for one second without hope. (Anonymous)

Faithful is he that calleth you, who also will do it. (1 Thess. 5:24)

In the early days of my ministry, while still in my dumb thirties (which immediately followed the stupid twenties), I was the senior pastor of a five-hundred-member church that my wife, Claudia, and I had started with a few families. Impressed? Don't be. The fact is that in spite of us, God grew that church into a solid group of folks with many new believers, some experienced saints, a Christian school, a radio outreach, and a small bus ministry. This was a genuine challenge for a guy from Memphis who had enrolled in college to become a cinematographer, received Christ as Savior in his junior year, and then said yes to God's call to preach. The duties, challenges, and trials of that growing church often caused me to wonder, "Will I survive the ministry?"

I have now served God in ministry for over thirty-five years. My wife and I planted two churches, which I pastored for eighteen years. We traveled the country for nine years in itinerant revival work while raising three children in a forty-foot-long hallway called an RV. In our present ministry, we help church planters establish new churches. We have, just like you, faced trials of the flesh, sickness, accidents, failure, rejection, misunderstanding, and disappointment. We have sometimes wept together and asked God to do something fresh in our hearts and in our ministry. While planting a church in Tennessee in the late 1990s, Claudia and I had several seasons of doubting God. Though the seasons were brief, I remember crying out, "Where are you, God? Have you forgotten us?" We have been tempted to quit more than once.

In spite of the negatives, we still press on, thoroughly enjoying the journey! We love the ministry. We love the challenges of asking God for daily bread, daily power, and daily leadership. We cherish the joys of learning new insights from His Word and new methods of helping others. We continue to press on. You can too.

If God has called you into ministry, it is His will that you survive. You can survive because God's grace is sufficient; because Jesus, Who lives in you, survived; and because God provides the means of survival.

God's Sufficient Grace

Recall the day God called you into ministry. That day was almost as significant as the day you became a Christian. When you turned from sin and put your trust for heaven in Christ alone (Rom. 10:13), He not only made you into a new creature (2 Cor. 2:14) but He also pledged to keep your soul for eternity (John 10:27–28). Biblical salvation is a work of the triune God. God the Father ordains, God the Son saves and declares righteous, and God the Holy Spirit convicts and draws a soul to Christ. The supernatural, saving work of our triune God cannot be negated. It is forever.

God's grace that keeps you in Him is the same grace that can keep you in the ministry—in spite of gossip, naysayers, physical ailments, your own doubts, and those irritating, often terrifyingly direct attacks of Satan. It was God's grace that drew you to Christ. It was God's grace that saved your soul. It is God's grace that keeps you safely in Him. And it will be God's grace that will lift you out of the slough of despond and energize you. In spite of what Satan the master liar says, you can press on. God's grace is necessary and sufficient for survival in ministry. It is all you need.

Jesus' Survival

You can survive because Jesus, Who lives in you, survived. God the Father called Jesus into ministry. His assignment was to become a man, keep the law, and die on the cross. As God in flesh, the Lord Jesus faced every trial and temptation that believers today face. Hebrews 4:15 says He was "in all points tempted like as we are, yet without sin." He was ridiculed, rejected, hated, lied about, betrayed, and arrested. He was laughed at, mocked, beaten, tortured, and nailed to a wooden cross, but still He pressed on with His mission. Things looked bad for our Savior, but we know the rest of the story!

On the third day Jesus conquered death. The stone was rolled away and the tomb was found empty. Jesus is alive! Our Savior is now pressing on, interceding for us at the right hand of the throne of God. The resurrection of Jesus Christ offers deliverance from hell for all who repent and believe, and His success in doing the Father's will makes victory over discouragement, depression, and doubt possible for all believers, including you.

Romans 6:6 promises that since you were crucified with Him, you are no longer a slave to sin. Though He did not ask you to physically share the whip or the nails or the cross, if you are in Christ, you were there with Him on the cross. By grace, you conquered death together. The power of the crucified and resurrected Christ is yours. You can ask and expect Him to lift you out of the hole of discouragement.

Are you tempted to trust your so-called spiritual self-efforts for encouragement? Do you say to yourself, "I just need to pray more, memorize more Bible verses, witness to more folks, and then I will be encouraged"? Those things are helpful. We all need to do more of them. However, simply by being in Christ you possess all the power you need to trust, be encouraged, and press on. Hudson Taylor discovered the blessing of being encouraged by the crucified Christ during his early years of ministry in China. In a letter to his sister, he said, "Here, I feel, is the secret: not asking how I am to get the sap out of the vine into myself, but remembering that Jesus is the Vine—the root, the stem, branches, twigs, leaves, flowers, fruit, all indeed. Aye, and far more too!"

Jesus Christ pressed on, is now pressing on, and will always be pressing on. So can you.

God's Means of Survival

You can survive because when God calls, He provides the means for survival. Noah was a survivor. For more than one hundred years, he endured mocking comments about his boat-building project. No rain had ever fallen from the sky, yet he was building one humongous boat. God had called him to the ministry of large boat production without power tools, duct tape, or Home Depot. That was a tall order. But since God gave the order, He provided the grace for Noah to survive. Maybe Noah tasted God's grace through heartening words from his wife. Maybe God spoke audibly to Noah as He did to Abraham. Whatever means God used to give Noah grace, it worked. Noah kept building. He finished his assignment and the rains came.

When the prophet Elijah prayed his "fire-come-down-from-heaven" prayer, God answered in a dramatic way, sending flames that humiliated the false prophets. At this peak of his prophetic career, Elijah may have thought the time had arrived to write a stirring autobiography detailing his noble accomplishments for Jehovah. But the next morning when Jezebel threatened to kill him, the great prophet couldn't take the heat from that fiery-tongued female. He ran like a clucking chicken into the desert, held a private pity party under a juniper tree, and asked God to take his life (1 Kings 19:4). God provided the means to encourage him: a long nap and an angel serving food and water. Elijah survived and pressed on.

Peter cursed and denied his Lord. Imagine his pain when the rooster crowed and he gazed into the eyes of Christ. Peter was ready to quit the ministry and get a job as a used car salesman (a fine job if you are in the will of God). However, God provided such forgiveness and restoration that only fifty days later, he preached a powerful sermon defending the Lord he had denied (Acts 2). At that Pentecost revival service three thousand souls believed. By God's grace, Peter survived.

Paul the apostle had one painful trial after another. He experienced hunger, nakedness, and shipwreck—and pressed on. He was whipped five times with thirty-nine stripes—and pressed on. Three times he was beaten with rods—and pressed on. He risked his life on rivers and oceans. He heard the murderous cries of mobs and was pummeled with rocks. He was ridiculed, rejected, lied about, and cursed. Paul had problems with an "assistant pastor," was betrayed by a businessman, and was jailed by several politicians. But God's grace was sufficient for Paul. He pressed on, thrived, and finished well (2 Tim. 4:7).

When I was a pastor, I often felt as if Sunday were a day on the mountaintop with Elijah followed by a Monday morning juniper-tree pity party. We might have had a wonderful day with large attendance, spiritual decisions, and the delicious icing on the cake—a great offering! In spite of my blessings, I would lose heart at the thought of a young couple who didn't attend, a member who complained, or a visitor who looked unhappy during the sermon. God never failed me, though. He was always faithful to send something or someone to encourage me. God had called me, and He provided daily grace. I pressed on, leaning on my life verse, 1 Thessalonians 5:24: "Faithful is he that calleth you, who also will do it."

This promise assures you and me that if God has called us as He called Noah, Elijah, Peter, and Paul, He will provide us with the means to endure. "Seeing we also are compassed about with so great a cloud of witnesses, let us lay aside every weight, and the sin which doth so easily beset us, and let us run with patience the race that is set before us" (Heb. 12:1). These men pressed on to their finish line, and so can you.

Sometimes you may wonder if you are going to reach that goal. You struggle with temptation from without and within. When I was a young man, I wondered if the temptations of the flesh would weaken when I got older. I now know that they do not. Thanks to biblical sanctification, each year I grow more sensitive to the power of the flesh, which I have learned does not improve with age. The flesh will plague each of us until we enter the presence of the perfect Savior. Satan, who is unwilling to grant days off from fleshly temptations, wants you to believe that ministry survival is impossible. But he is, as always, wrong! Satan is a liar. You can survive. You will not survive because you are clever, capable, gifted, or self-motivated, with influential personal contacts, a great heritage, and remarkable abilities. You can survive in spite of being sinful, prone to walking in the flesh, and a big fat zero without God (Matt. 5:3). God's never-failing love that has called you to the exalted task of ministry will provide all the grace you need.

Pilgrim, don't be surprised by potholes in the road along life's short trip. I am still learning and certainly don't have all the answers. But I do know this: God's grace is incomprehensibly sufficient, and multitudes of others have finished well. Though we are just dumb sheep following a wise Shepherd, we too can press on!

Living Chapter 1

1. Memorize 1 Thessalonians 5:24, “Faithful is he that calleth you, who also will do it.”

2. Make a 1 Thessalonians 5:24 placard to hang where you will see it every morning (on your refrigerator door, your bathroom mirror, or auto rear-view mirror).

3. Believe that God, Who called you, will give you the grace to press on.

PRESS *ON!*

. . . SUCCESS IS CLOSER THAN YOU THINK

2

Success is simple. Do what's right, the right way, at the right time. (Andrew Glasgow)

Moreover it is required in stewards that a man be found faithful. (1 Cor. 4:2)

Success is not an evil word. God wants us to reach for it and enjoy it! When Joshua was chosen to lead the Israelites into Canaan, God told him to "meditate therein [the Word of God] day and night . . . then thou shalt make thy way prosperous, and then thou shalt have good success" (Josh. 1:8). God was speaking of spiritual success that glorifies Him, not worldly success that exalts self. The world tries to convince us that success belongs only to those who are famous, attractive, and wealthy. Radio, television, movies, magazines, and newspapers shout, "Be famous, be beautiful, be rich—that is success!"

Perhaps your parents raised you to believe that success is being at the top of your class in school or at the peak of your profession. Of course you want to do your best for God, but if you spend your life trying to always be The Best, you will struggle with frustration and feelings of inferiority; for no matter how skilled you become, you will always be able to find a better teacher, writer, farmer, engineer—or preacher—than you are.

The good news is that Christian success has nothing at all to do with looks, peer approval, bank accounts, or even college degrees. Biblical success is simply pleasing God by faithfully doing what He wants you to do. "And the world passeth away, and the lust thereof: but he that doeth the will of God abideth for ever" (1 John 2:17). "Moreover it is required in stewards, that a man be found faithful" (1 Cor. 4:2). At this moment, you are probably more successful than you realize.

Failure Is Painful

Satan, the great accuser, labors to charge you with failure (Rev. 12:10). He whispers that you should be reaching more new people through your evangelism and be more effective in your counseling. He insinuates that you are a failure in your struggle with personal sin, that you are an ineffective leader and a poor husband and father.

He knows that it is painful to feel like a failure. Failure comes in a variety of bitter flavors. It may be that punch-in-the-stomach ache you feel when a church member offers "constructive criticism" as you walk toward the pulpit to preach. It could be the knife-between-the-shoulder-blades pain of overhearing harsh words about your children. Then there is the kick-in-the-gut agony that arrives with the phone call from an influential church member who announces he is leaving the church with his family of twelve because they are "not being fed." We've all been there.

Elijah's preaching infuriated Jezebel, throwing that bold prophet into a panic. He then became so discouraged that he told God that he was ready to die (1 Kings 19:4). Those self-destructive thoughts came from the heart of a man who felt like a failure. After the Israelites failed to get Solomon's temple rebuilt for about fifteen years, God sent the prophet Haggai to challenge them to get back to work. As they observed the Feast of Tabernacles, they remembered how God had miraculously delivered their forefathers from bondage. In comparison, they had made poor progress in simply rebuilding the temple. Their failure had turned them into cowards (Hag. 2:5). Much later, Peter hurt so much after his denial that he cried bitter tears (Matt. 26:75).

When you feel like a failure in the ministry, you may hurt so badly that you become afraid of people, afraid of the future, afraid of more failure—maybe even afraid of going to church. Failure, even the fear of failure, is painful.

One Nice Dog

As a college freshman, I learned much about rejection and failure during my attempt to sell books door-to-door. The sales recruiter offered me a near-guarantee that I'd make enough money to pay a year of college tuition—maybe even to buy a new Corvette! My assignment was to sell the *Nave's Topical Bible* and the *Wycliffe Bible Commentary* in Iowa City, Iowa. I did not have loads of fun or make piles of cash. The folks in that secular-minded college town were not one bit interested in my Bible-related books. I lasted for three painful weeks.

On a horribly hot June afternoon, I approached a house, knocked on the door, and turned around to face the front yard. (My sales-school instructors taught that it is offensive to peer through the front door of a stranger's house. If you have your back to him when he opens the door, he feels less threatened and more in control.) I patiently waited. No one came to the door. I knocked again—a little louder. Still no response.

"This has been one hard day," I whined to myself. "Slammed doors, unfriendly people. My total sales are zero. I am hot, tired, discouraged, and getting angry." After looking around at the deserted neighborhood, I pounded on the door again. Wham! Wham! No answer. A little louder. Wham! Wham! Still no answer.

Then I saw him. Curled up in the corner of the porch was a furry, brown, friendly dog. I think he was smiling. I glanced both ways to see if anyone was watching. Satisfied that it was just me and Mr. Dog, I sat down on the front step and called him over. The dog got up and lazily loped over to me. When he was seated and comfortable, I took my *Nave's Topical Bible* out of my sales kit and gave him my entire sales demonstration.

"Look here, Mr. Dog, you can use this amazing *Nave's Topical Bible* to look up the word *wife*. You, my canine friend, can discover all the Bible has to say about your doggie spouse. You can choose any other word or topic that interests you. This helpful tool will guide you in your quest for truth."

I then proudly showed him my *Wycliffe Bible Commentary*, dutifully warning Mr. Dog about the references to theistic evolution in chapter 1. During the entire sales demonstration, this intelligent canine paid close attention and wagged his tail enthusiastically, panting at my every word. He also had a lovely smile—in spite of his breath. Mr. Dog did not buy my books. He was polite about it, but he still did not buy. More rejection on that hot day.

A week later I quit that job and rode a Greyhound bus to my home in Memphis, feeling like a failure. But then one of my dad's friends introduced me to the Bernzomatic Fire Detection System . . . "You can hear its fog-horn alarm one-quarter mile away!" The sales method was simple: show up on the porch with your movie projector in hand, smile brightly and ask if you could show your ten-minute movie about fire safety. This "safety" film, complete with alarming images and loud sirens wailing in the background, was narrated by a professional announcer who soberly listed terrifying facts about how hot a burning room gets in one minute, how poison gases usually kill you before the flames, and how the Bernzomatic Corporation was committed to helping your family escape a raging inferno. It was just plain scary. I sold many alarms that summer and made enough money to go back to college in the fall.

I also learned a lesson that has helped me through many ministry challenges and mistakes. It has consistently led me from failure to victory, from pain to peace. That lesson is this: You can fail and not be a failure.

You Can Fail and Not Be a Failure

We are taught from childhood that failure is disgraceful. We used to say, "Our team lost the game . . . I forgot my recital piece . . . I was the last one picked for the team." Now we say, "His church is large and prosperous while we are still struggling in a dreary storefront."

Those sentiments and others reflect what we have been taught to call failure. Worse than that, we have learned that success means we are good and failure, bad. Maybe you have believed that. I have good news for you: you can fail and not be a failure. An effective salesman knows that in order to be a success, in order to make a sale, he must talk to many folks who will say no to his offer. Many noes eventually lead to the yeses of success.

Can you think of someone who flunked out of one ministry, faltered in another, but finally found his position of effective service? He learned that you can fail and not be a failure. Anytime you choose to sin, you fail. But if you confess that sin, enjoy forgiveness, and move on, you are not a failure. You may fail to love others, fail to pray, fail to spend time with your children, or fail to reach your ministry goals. A person who is a failure lets failure hinder and even halt his spiritual growth. But if you will be honest about your sin, open to learning from your experience (which may reveal a need to pursue other goals or ambitions), you are not a failure. Ignore the world's definition of success. Be faithful to your calling.

Success Is Faithfulness

In the eyes of the world, Noah failed for more than 120 years. What kind of man, you ask, would dedicate his life to faithfully building a massive boat on dry land where rain had never fallen? Noah looked like an idiot and a failure. But his years of patient endurance led to the preservation of the human race.

Jeremiah the prophet spent his life preaching a message of God's judgment to Judah. God ordained him as a prophet in his mother's womb! While pursuing his calling, he was persecuted by his own family, the townspeople of Anathoth, and the entire nation of Judah. He faithfully warned of God's coming judgment for about forty years, but few listened. When this warning prophet realized that his message was being ignored, he became the weeping prophet.

Jeremiah looked and felt like a failure, but in God's eyes he was a success—for he simply did what he was called to do. In the middle of the book of Lamentations, while crying over the destruction of Jerusalem, Jeremiah sounded a triumphant note of hope. "It is of the LORD's mercies that we are not consumed, because his compassions fail not. They are new every morning: great is thy faithfulness" (Lam. 3:22–23).

If, as theologians say, God's primary attribute is His holiness, His faithfulness is surely a close second. "Kings shall see and arise, princes also shall worship, because of the LORD that is faithful" (Isa. 49:7). Jeremiah measured God's greatness by His faithfulness. He knew that God would be quick to forgive and restore Judah the moment she repented. Could it be that this weeping preacher had peace about his ultimate success in ministry because he knew His faithful God valued steadfastness above results?

Success Is Stewardship

A Christian is a steward, or keeper, of God's accounts. God has entrusted you with all that you have: time, spiritual gifts, money, family, ministry (James 1:17). All He asks is for you to be faithful with His accounts. "Let a man so account of us, as of the ministers of Christ, and stewards of the mysteries of God. Moreover it is required in stewards, that a man be found faithful" (1 Cor. 4:1–2). In the parable of the talents, the master gave money to each of his three servants. Two of the servants were faithful to invest and grow the master's account. When the master returned from his journey, he praised those two faithful stewards: "Well done, thou good and faithful servant: thou hast been faithful over a few things, I will make thee ruler over many things" (Matt. 25:21). What the lord does not say is revealing. He does not say, "Well done, wealthy servant," or "handsome, talented, popular, and famous servant." Just like that earthly master, all your Master asks is for you to diligently manage His accounts. Faithful stewardship equals success.

Stop comparing yourself to others (2 Cor. 10:12). Stop evaluating your success with the world's measuring tape of fame, fortune, physical appearance, church size, or acclaim of your peers. Simply be faithful. Be faithful in prayer, in Bible study, in evangelism, in pursuit of holiness, in ministry of the Word, in your God-given duties.

Kent and Barbara Hughes's book *Liberating Ministry from the Success Syndrome* is a scriptural and encouraging study of "success" in the ministry. Kent points out a time in his ministry when he wanted to quit because of deep feelings of failure. From the time he preached his first sermon as a sixteen–year-old, people had said he would do great things for God. From those expectations he built a false concept of success, and when he failed to reach his self-imposed criteria, he wanted to quit. He writes that God does not require His servants to be outwardly successful but instead that they be faithful, loving, prayerful, living by faith, and striving for holiness.

The Hugheses' book offers these soul-searching questions. They suggest that you get away to a private place, prayerfully set yourself before God, and answer them as if they were heard in the voice of God.

1. Are you proving faithful in the exercise of your ministry? Specifically, are you obedient to God's Word? Or is there, perhaps, some area, in personal or public ministry, in which you are knowingly disobedient?

2. Are you living your life as a servant, or have you drifted from servanthood into self-service? This question is fundamental to success, for this will move you from success to failure.

3. Do you love God? There can be no success without loving God.

4. Do you believe that God's Son is the Creator of everything in the universe, sustainer of every atom, the goal of all creation, and the lover of our souls who died for us?

5. Are you a person of prayer? Do you regularly take significant portions of time for exposure to God, to bear your needs and the needs of your people to God?

6. Is your life growing in holiness, or are you captive to culture? In respect to holiness, would God classify your life a success or a failure? This question is so important to the Christian life and ministry that it must be answered.

7. What is your basic attitude toward your ministry—positive or negative? Negative people never fully experience success, regardless of accomplishments. Their negativism taints their work for God and the experience of satisfaction they might have enjoyed.[1]

---

1. Kent and Barbara Hughes. *Liberating Ministry from the Success Syndrome* (Wheaton, Ill.: Tyndale House, 1987), 109-10.

Your success has nothing to do with what others in ministry are accomplishing. It is determined by whether you are faithfully doing what He has called you to do. You probably have told your children not to worry about smart students in their classes who claim never to study but still make A's. "Don't compare yourself with the brain in the class," you say encouragingly. "Just study hard and do your best. That is all God expects." That is good counsel. Why not follow it yourself? Reject Satan's accusations that you are a failure because your accomplishments appear less significant than those of others. Determine what God wants you to do at this moment, and do it. That is success.

Living Chapter 2

1. Get alone with God and honestly answer Hugheses' seven questions.

2. Search the word *faithful* in your Bible study software or concordance. Print the list and study one verse a day during your devotions.

3. Write down a one-word Bible definition of success.

4. Prayerfully meditate on the following verses.

> Know therefore that the LORD thy God, he is God, the faithful God, which keepeth covenant and mercy with them that love him and keep his commandments to a thousand generations. (Deut. 7:9)
>
> That I gave my brother Hanani, and Hananiah the ruler of the palace, charge over Jerusalem: for he was a faithful man, and feared God above many. (Neh. 7:2)
>
> O love the LORD, all ye his saints: for the LORD preserveth the faithful, and plentifully rewardeth the proud doer. (Ps. 31:23)
>
> Mine eyes shall be upon the faithful of the land, that they may dwell with me: he that walketh in a perfect way, he shall serve me. (Ps. 101:6)
>
> Most men will proclaim every one his own goodness: but a faithful man who can find? (Prov. 20:6)
>
> A faithful man shall abound with blessings: but he that maketh haste to be rich shall not be innocent. (Prov. 28:20)

As ye also learned of Epaphras our dear fellowservant, who is for you a faithful minister of Christ. (Col. 1:7)

And I thank Christ Jesus our Lord, who hath enabled me, for that he counted me faithful, putting me into the ministry. (1 Tim. 1:12)

And the things that thou hast heard of me among many witnesses, the same commit thou to faithful men, who shall be able to teach others also. (2 Tim. 2:2)

PRESS *ON!*

. . . FIND PEACE IN LONELINESS

Loneliness is about the scariest thing there is. (Anonymous)

Thrice was I beaten with rods, once was I stoned, thrice I suffered shipwreck, a night and a day I have been in the deep; in journeyings often, in perils of waters, in perils of robbers, in perils by mine own countrymen, in perils by the heathen, in perils in the city, in perils in the wilderness, in perils in the sea, in perils among false brethren. (2 Cor. 11:25–26)

It was a hot Southern summer day, but still it was easy to listen. The speaker was an aged and veteran pastor, whose assignment was to motivate and challenge a classroom full of preachers. His speech was labored, sounding like a grinding cement mixer. I suspect he was in pain, since he suffered from Parkinson's disease, but he spoke with fervency, revealing his burden for God's servants—those heroes who labor in full-time ministry.

"You say you have problems?" he barked. "Did Paul have problems? You bet! He had plenty of them! It is normal to have problems in the ministry. If you are bitter at God because you have problems, you may not belong in the ministry." As he spoke, he fit the apostle Paul's arduous life and heart-pounding problems into a frame like pieces of a puzzle, which are crooked and gnarled but eventually form a remarkable picture.

Second Corinthians is Paul's vindication of his ministry. In this *Apologia Pro Vita Sua* ("Defense of His Life"), Paul bared his soul. He warned about the ritualistic legalism of the Judaizers, who used skilled rhetoric to accuse Paul of being dishonest, spiritually weak, and a poor preacher. (Has that ever happened to you?) He then defended his calling, authority, and motives, reminding the Corinthians that he had endured perils ("exposure to harm or injury, something that can cause harm," from the Latin root for *danger*) for their sake. Second Corinthians 11 lists his hardships: beatings, stoning, shipwrecks, dangerous journeys on land and sea, robberies, and personal assaults. Paul regularly faced dangers, but he survived and pressed on for the sake of his people.

Amazingly, he was even thankful for those trials: "Thanks be unto God, which always causeth us to triumph in Christ" (2 Cor. 2:14). Paul went on to say, "I take pleasure in infirmities, in reproaches, in necessities, in persecutions, in distresses for Christ's sake" (2 Cor. 12:10). You too can be thankful for trials if you will see them as normal and as tools that God uses to shape you into His image.

Let's look at common ministry perils: loneliness, discouragement (chapter 4), and temptation (chapter 5). Of course there are more perils than these, but these three are direct attacks on the mind. Satan knows that if he can get through the door of your mind and mold your thinking, sinful actions may soon follow.

A Peril Called Loneliness

A lonely man walked into his doctor's office and said, "Doctor, Doctor, will you please split my personality? I'm lonely and need someone to talk to." Another man placed an ad in a Kansas newspaper saying, "For five dollars I will listen to you talk for a half an hour without comment." He was soon overwhelmed by ten to twenty calls a day! According to Dr. Leonard Canner, a veteran psychiatrist who specializes in depression, "The human being is the only species that can't survive alone. Every human needs another human . . . otherwise he's dead. A telephone call to a depressed person can save a life. An occasional word, a ten-minute visit, can be more effective than twenty-four hours of nursing care. You can buy nursing care, but you can't buy love."

Jesus tasted loneliness on earth. He willingly became flesh and "was made in the likeness of men" (Phil. 2:7). As a man, He endured hunger (Matt. 4:2), felt compassion (Matt. 9:36), battled temptation (Matt. 4:1), and experienced loneliness. He probably felt alone as a child and teenager when He sat in the synagogue and submitted to religious instruction or listened humbly to Joseph's lessons on using carpentry tools. Christ was lonely when He preached to followers who did not understand Him and sat through trials for crimes He did not commit. Jesus was lonely when He was arrested and His disciples deserted Him. Our Savior endured the loneliest hours in history while hanging on the cross, forsaken by the Father. Christ was tempted in all points as we are—including in loneliness.

Loneliness and solitude are different. Solitude is voluntary. You may choose to come away from others for a while to meditate, reflect, or simply rest from social interaction. Solitude can be refreshing. Loneliness, instead, is forced upon you. It can be draining, defeating, and depressing and may lead to feelings of worthlessness and rejection. In creation, the first thing that God said was "not good" was loneliness. He created Eve for Adam because it was "not good that man should be alone" (Gen. 2:18). Since creation, humans have needed the company of others.

One of Satan's most subtle tools against a pastor is loneliness. If he can convince you that you are a lone, unique sufferer, the only struggling prophet left on earth, he has an advantage over you. He may convince you that no one understands—that no one *can* understand. But whatever your trial, it is not unique: "There hath no temptation taken you but such as is common to man" (1 Cor. 10:13). "Resist [the Devil] . . . knowing that the same afflictions are accomplished in your brethren that are in the world" (1 Pet. 5:9). No matter what you are facing, you are not alone. Some brother in ministry somewhere on earth is facing the same temptation. You are not a ministry Lone Ranger!

My wife and I have planted churches and now assist men who do that work. We know from experience that pastors, and especially church planters, are often lonely. Church planters may struggle with lack of fellowship in the early days of a new work. They do not have staff members with whom to talk, pray, and fellowship. The church planter's wife is particularly open to feelings of despair and loneliness because of a dearth of like-minded ministry wives in her town.

This kind of loneliness is not a sin, but it often sets the stage for sin, so it needs to be dealt with. There is no quick fix or any guarantee that by reading this chapter you will suddenly conquer this difficulty. I do not have a sure-fire solution for loneliness. But I can offer some suggestions to help you manage, endure, and even benefit from loneliness. Let's look at two common sources of loneliness and then examine six steps to victory.

Your Convictions May Produce Loneliness

If you are committed to believing, preaching, and living the whole counsel of God, your convictions will probably make you a loner, or at least make you feel like one. You can be in a crowd of preachers and feel alone. Simply believing in and preaching the true gospel (1 Cor. 15:3–4) may cause isolation, for there surely will be pastors in your city who preach salvation by works rather than faith. Your practical applications of truth may be different from those of other pastors. Men in ministry have differences of opinion in areas of practical Christian living—preaching and music styles, entertainment, child-rearing, evangelism, and so forth. Though you have formed your convictions through careful study of God's Word, not everyone will agree. As you follow your convictions without compromise, those convictions may lead to loneliness.

Your Position May Produce Loneliness

Leaders are often lonely. I speak from pastoral experience. A pastor's relationship with those to whom he preaches must be as shepherd to sheep rather than as friend to buddy. Though he loves each one, he has to maintain a bit of professional distance from his people. He must avoid getting so close to one person or family that others sense favoritism or unequal affection.

A pastor must also work to be a cheerleader with a positive vision, constantly encouraging his people that the future is bright. He cannot often afford to be down, discouraged, and negative. But at the end of a difficult day filled with heavy ministry problems, he may need to talk to someone. Though a pastor and his wife share most confidences, he may sense that a certain situation or conflict may alter her feelings toward a church member, and her otherwise helpful, sensitive heart may even react with a spirit of bitterness. If he decides, therefore, to carry his burden alone, Satan says, "This is not fair! God has left you all alone!" The evil one takes advantage of a pastor who is alone—or feels that he is.

A pastor of any size church must strive to stay closer to God than anyone else in the church. He cannot lead folks any further spiritually than he is. As he strives to stay ahead of his congregation, he may feel the lack of an understanding friend to fellowship with or a mentor to confide in. Satan will work to convince him that a lonely position of leadership is not worth the pain.

Ministry loneliness is common, real, and discouraging. It often seems unfair. But it is actually a good gift from God, Who is eager to protect His chosen servants. With His help, you can maintain, tolerate, and even enjoy loneliness!

You Can Conquer Loneliness

1. Accept circumstances that cannot be changed.

The apostle Paul said, "I have learned, in whatsoever state I am, therewith to be content" (Phil. 4:11). He was not referring to a state like Georgia, Tennessee, or California. He was saying that he had learned to be content in any circumstance that his good God brought his way. That's an amazing statement, considering that Paul faced countless situations of loneliness, hatred, and rejection. What was the source of His contentment? Definitely not his feelings. Paul's contentment was anchored to facts, not emotions. He knew that God was with him in the desert, in prison, in storms at sea, during beatings, while being stoned, during court trials, while facing angry mobs, and as a lonely prisoner in a Roman dungeon.

If God has ordained that you live with loneliness, are you willing to joyfully do His will?

Has God placed you in a high, and therefore lonely, position of Christian leadership? Is that limelight something you don't enjoy or need? Are you surrounded by people all the time but feel lonely in the crowd? I am not minimizing your pain, but remember that God does say to "be content with such things as ye have: for he hath said, I will never leave thee, nor forsake thee" (Heb. 13:5). Are you willing to accept God-ordained circumstances—even loneliness—if they will bring utmost glory to your Redeemer?

Learning to be content all circumstances takes time and experience. God may use loneliness to teach you something some Christians do not learn in a lifetime—to be content in God alone.

2. Let loneliness remind you to be grateful.

Loneliness may produce in you a spirit of thanksgiving. When loneliness seeks to overwhelm you, say no to your dark thoughts and doubts. Instead, pray through a mental list of things for which you are thankful. You may be alone, but you are in Christ, forever protected from the penalty of sin. You may be alone, but Satan is limited in how much he may torment you (just like Job). You are now alone, but heroic saints have gone before you who accomplished much for God while being alone. You may be alone, but a cloud of witnesses in heaven is watching over you, observing your willingness to walk alone that God may be glorified (Heb. 12:1). A grateful heart can see light in the darkest room.

3. Remember that you are never really alone.

God often reminded His servants that He would always be with them. On Jacob's solitary journey to find a wife, God gave him a heavenly dream of a ladder reaching to heaven (Gen. 28). The voice of the Lord assured him that He would fulfill His promise to give him the land of promise. He said that his family and descendants would multiply and be blessed. God then told Jacob that He would stay with him until He had fulfilled His promise. "Behold, I am with thee, and will keep thee in all places whither thou goest, and will bring thee again into this land; for I will not leave thee, until I have done that which I have spoken to thee of" (Gen. 28:15). That same promise is yours. God has a plan for you and your ministry. He will be with you until He is finished with you.

In the first eight verses of Deuteronomy 31, Moses assured Israel of God's presence and commended Joshua to them as a leader. He said to Israel, "Be strong and of a good courage, fear not, nor be afraid of them: for the LORD thy God, he it is that doth go with thee; he will not fail thee, nor forsake thee" (Deut. 31:6). Moses immediately turned to Joshua and repeated the promise: "And the LORD, he it is that doth go before thee; he will be with thee, he will not fail thee, neither forsake thee: fear not, neither be dismayed" (Deut. 31:8). When Joshua took over after Moses died, God reminded Him that He would always be with him: "There shall not any man be able to stand before thee all the days of thy life: as I was with Moses, so I will be with thee: I will not fail thee, nor forsake thee" (Josh. 1:5).

When Elijah complained to God that he was the only faithful prophet in left in Israel, God reminded him that he was not all alone. "Yet I have left me seven thousand in Israel, all the knees which have not bowed unto Baal, and every mouth which hath not kissed him" (1 Kings 19:18). There were others out there also standing "alone" and feeling lonely. Joseph grew closer to God when he was alone in prison than when he was second in command under Pharaoh. Daniel's faith grew in the den of lions, where he was certainly not alone. Your God, Who never slumbers nor sleeps, will never leave you all alone.

Though you may feel alone, you are not. Your body is the temple of the Holy Spirit (1 Cor. 6:19), so as long as you have your body with you, God is there! He is just as much with you in your darkest hour of loneliness as when you are in the light of many friends.

4. Make your wife and family your best friends.

Claudia and I married in 1973. When God put us together, we became one. She is my best friend on earth. Most of the time when she leaves the room, I am lonely. God said, "It is not good that man should be alone; I will make him an help meet for him" (Gen. 2:18). The Hebrew word for meet, *neged*, conveys the idea of a counterpart. Your wife is your counterpart, or completer. That may be one of the reasons God requires a pastor to be married (1 Tim. 3:2), for He knows the power of loneliness, and a God-given wife helps the husband have victory over it. A pastor who conquers loneliness is usually enjoying the God-given friendship and protection of his wife. He feels incomplete without her. Make your wife your best friend—your closest companion. Talk with her. Share your burdens. Pray together. Don't let Satan make you enemies.

Treasure your children. They grow up and leave the nest in a moment. Cherish the season of life when you can enjoy their company. Read to them, relax with them, discover with them. I learn much while reading books written for children! When I pastored a busy church in Wisconsin, one of our favorite (and cheap) family times was to spend Saturday afternoon together at the local library. Another memorable (and yummy) ritual was sharing a pizza after the Sunday evening service. Field trips, backyard campfires, picnics, and the weekly day off spent with family can help ease your loneliness. Those memories also become valuable investments in your future friendships with your children. In later years when they are grown, you will be thankful for every minute you enjoyed with them.

Are you a church planter or the pastor of a small work? You are likely to have more family time in the early years of your church than later, when responsibilities and challenges may increase with a growing congregation. These can be wonderful years to grow close to your family. Organize your time wisely to take advantage of your less-demanding schedule. Develop friendships within your own family. You can prevent loneliness by treasuring and strengthening family ties.

5. Find a friend or mentor to provide companionship.

Friendship is a loneliness poultice that our Great Physician applies when needed. Apply friendship generously to your aching heart and enjoy instant relief. Develop at least one true friendship. A true friend will love you when you are not so lovable (Prov. 17:17). A friend will tell you the truth about yourself (Prov. 27:6). A friend may stick closer to you than your own brother (Prov. 18:24). A friend will help you grow into the image of Christ (Prov. 27:17). Sometimes God wants you to be alone to personally enjoy His friendship, like Moses did for forty years in the desert or like Joseph did in prison. But many times He provides a Jonathan for a lonely David, a Barnabas to cheer up the persecuted Paul, or a Lazarus to be a friend of Jesus (remember that Jesus cried when Lazarus died).

Today, people do not even have to live near you to be your true friends. My wife and I live on the road in our fifth-wheel trailer. As church-planting helpers, we are never really at home. We spend about six months with each pastor to help start the church and then move to another city to help another couple. We stay long enough to make wonderful friends and fall in love with a new congregation, and then we say goodbye. Sometimes we whine to one another about being lonely, but that is rare. Most of the time, we are not lonely. Is that because we are best friends? Not entirely. We do have one another, but we also have many friends around the world. We can communicate with those friends in a moment via telephone or our computers.

I love/hate computers. I love them when they work. I do not love them when they seem to be demon-possessed. When I was young, Spam was a "miracle meat in a can." I preferred that it stay there. Computer spam is a persistent, unavoidable irritant—one of a plethora of computing perils. However, in spite of those frustrations, Claudia and I use our computers daily. We use them to do ministry and to connect with our friends and loved ones. They help dispel our loneliness.

To conquer loneliness, benefit from e-communication and phone fellowship. Connect with like-minded pastors to share news, needs, and even complaints. Ministry problems are not unique. Do not allow Satan to take advantage of you with his "you-are-all-alone-and-should-feel-sorry-for-yourself" ruse. You may want to request our *Press On!* newsletter, join our blog, or sign up for Claudia's encouraging "Monday Morning Club" at www.ipresson.com.

6. Read inspiring Christian biographies.

When my family and I left itinerant evangelistic work in 1995 to start a new church in Franklin, Tennessee, we knew it would be a challenge. Franklin is a suburb of Nashville—home to over eight hundred Baptist churches. We started that church almost twenty years after our first church plant in Wisconsin. Times had changed!

During that tough time, I leaned heavily on my habit of starting each day alone with God in His Word. To my regular Bible study and prayer, I added the reading of ministry-servant biographies. An account of the life of missionary Hudson Taylor, *Hudson Taylor's Spiritual Secret*, became a secret to my perseverance and mental health. I read about his sacrifice, lack of living quarters for his family, cultural challenges, and threat of physical harm. I read of his being cold, homeless, and without friends in a strange land. In spite of his hardships, Taylor pressed on, stayed close to God, and built a successful team of missionaries. "If Taylor can go to a foreign land with no guarantee of income, housing, or acceptance among the people," I thought to myself, "then why should I complain? I have financial support, a place to live, a field of service, and a family that loves me. I think I will just go ahead and press on through another day!"

Claudia and I have been wonderfully challenged and encouraged by missionary biographies. God directs us to those we need. We have rejoiced in and been rebuked by the spirit of sacrifice, hunger to know God, and daily live-by-faith attitudes of C. T. Studd, J. O. Fraser, and George Mueller. We have read how God takes His chosen servants through loneliness to prepare them to do His work. By letting them be alone on the backside of the desert, in a foreign city with a hostile culture, or in a cold, damp prison, God teaches His servants that He will always be with them. Loneliness seems to be one of God's essential training tools for effectiveness in ministry.

You and I have the same God as these men who kept on doing the will of God in spite of opposition and lonely times. Your trials may not be as severe as theirs (1 have not lost children and several wives like missionary Adoniram Judson), but you have access to the same miraculous power. Read about them. Underline passages that the Holy Spirit applies to your heart. Escape to the world of a dedicated servant of God and rejoice that you have the same God . . . just different circumstances! Your loneliness does not mean that you are out of the will of God, that you are living in sin, or that God has forgotten you. It is simply one way God is stirring you to pray with fervency, to seek to know Him better, and to depend on Him alone.

Living Chapter 3

1. Read *Hudson Taylor's Spiritual Secret.*

2. Every time you pray in private, thank God that you are never really alone.

3. Email or call a friend in ministry who may be as lonely as you.

4. Stop feeling sorry for yourself and find someone to encourage and help.

5. Call a friend in ministry and tell him one thing you learned from this chapter. Suggest that you communicate with one another often.

6. Read one of our favorite ministry biographies.

   Mountain Rain (the story of J. O. Fraser) by Eileen Crossman

   C. T. Studd: Cricketer and Pioneer by Norman Grubbs

   George Mueller of Bristol by A. T. Pierson

PRESS *ON!*

. . . THROUGH DISCOURAGEMENT

4

Many of the great achievements of the world were accomplished by tired and discouraged men who kept on working. (Source unknown)

Be of good courage, and he shall strengthen your heart, all ye that hope in the LORD. (Ps. 31:24)

At the end of a difficult day in church-planting, Claudia said, "David, I believe that the church planter's biggest enemy is not the compromising church across town or the carnal church member, or even the unseen forces of evil. It is discouragement." I heartily agree with my wife.

The word *discouragement* is formed from the Latin prefix *dis-*, meaning "opposite or reverse" and *courage*. Courage is bravery, seen in David who confronted Goliath, Daniel who slept in the den of lions, or pastors who preach the whole counsel of God. Discouragement, then, is the reverse of courage—and that is fear. If you are discouraged, you are fearful. Is it God's will for you to live in fear?

Paul told Timothy, "God hath not given us the spirit of fear, but of power, and of love, and of a sound mind" (2 Tim. 1:7). If God does not give the spirit of fear, it's obvious where it comes from. If you are discouraged in your battle with Satan, you will have trouble praying. You will lose confidence in God, question your spiritual worth, and maybe even doubt your salvation.

Charles Spurgeon, though known as the prince of preachers, was still disposed to severe discouragement that bordered on depression. He said in his sermon "When the Preacher Is Downcast," "Fits of depression come over the most of us. Cheerful as we may be, we must at intervals be cast down. The strong are not always vigorous, the wise not always ready, the brave not always courageous, and the joyous not always happy." Jeremiah knew discouragement when he had preached over forty years with little response. He tried even to quit the ministry, saying in Jeremiah 20:7, 9, "I am in derision daily, every one mocketh me. . . . I will not make mention of him, nor speak any more in his name." But since Jeremiah was ordained to the ministry by God (just like you), he couldn't quit. "But his word was in mine heart as a burning fire shut up in my bones . . . and I could not stay" (Jer. 20:9). Discouragement in ministry is real, it is common, and it can be devastating. However, you can conquer this foe. Since God has not given you the spirit of fear, He will give you the tools to take courage.

Those tools are found in a sermon preached by the prophet Haggai. In 586 BC, God chastened the Israelites by allowing Nebuchadnezzar to invade their land, tear down Solomon's temple, and take them into captivity. About forty years later, Cyrus decreed that they could return to their beloved Jerusalem to rebuild the temple. A remnant returned, but they were habitual procrastinators (Hag. 1:2). For about sixteen years they failed to get the job done, so God sent Haggai and Zechariah to motivate them. The book of Haggai records four sermons intended to get the people back to work. God used Haggai's sermon in chapter 1, and the people resumed work on the temple. However, in chapter 2, they appeared weak, fearful, and discouraged (vv. 4–5). In 2:1–9, Haggai preached a powerful message of encouragement, pointing out common causes of discouragement and offering a four-point plan to have victory over it.

Common Causes of Discouragement

Guilt

Guilt can cause discouragement. In Haggai's first sermon, he rebuked the Israelites for spending much time on their own houses while taking little time on God's house (1:4) and challenged them to "go up to the mountain, and bring wood, and build the house" (1:8). Even though they had responded to the charge and resumed work on the temple (1:14), they still struggled because of God's lingering judgment (Hag. 2:10–19). With three rhetorical questions, Haggai declared the obvious—that the temple they were building was inferior to Solomon's temple—a statement that likely increased the pain of their guilt (2:3; cf. Ezra 3:12–13).

Guilt because of sin is discouraging. I detect a tone of despair in Paul's voice when he said, "For I know that in me (that is, in my flesh,) dwelleth no good thing: for to will is present with me; but how to perform that which is good I find not" (Rom. 7:18). The moment you sin, Satan speaks up. You may enter an evil place, speak a hurtful word, or think an ungodly thought. No matter what the sin, Satan responds. The malicious accuser (Rev. 12:10) whispers, "Who do think you are, trying to pray, preach, lead, or serve God? You cannot go one hour without disloyalty to the Lord you claim to love. You may as well quit the ministry, O phony one!" The good news is that God forgives, restores, and revives those who are honest about sin and willing to confess (1 John 1:9). If you are discouraged because of unconfessed sin, pause now to settle it with God. He is always willing to restore your courage.

Failure

Feelings of failure give birth to defeat and discouragement. Each discourse of Haggai opens with the Hebrew calendar date it was preached. Haggai's sermon on discouragement was delivered "in the seventh month, on the one and twentieth day of the month" (2:1). The twenty-first day of Tishri (our October/November) was the eighth day, or end, of the observance of the Feast of Tabernacles (Booths). While remembering God's care for their forefathers during the wilderness wandering, the Israelites felt like bumbling failures because they had not rebuilt the temple.

Elijah felt like a failure and even had thoughts of suicide when Jezebel turned against him (1 Kings 19:2–4). Peter felt like a failure after denying the Savior and wept in bitter discouragement when the crowing rooster confirmed his failure (Matt. 26:75).

A myriad of circumstances lead to feelings of failure. You may spend hours preparing a sermon that in your humble opinion may spark nationwide revival. But feelings of failure descend as you see folks snoozing during your delivery. Your heavenly vision of a new program that "will absolutely revitalize our church" is rejected by the deacons. Your wife may fail to live up to others' standards of child-rearing or Bible teaching or pastor's wife decorum (whatever that is). When I pastored, I felt like quitting when after spending months discipling new believers, they left our church in favor of a high-entertainment, low-commitment church.

Of course, some things that appear to be failures are not. They may be a result of wrong expectations or an inaccurate comparison of yourself or your ministry to others. But whether real or perceived, failure can be emotionally weakening, spiritually devastating, and mentally depressing. It is a frequent cause of discouragement.

People

Another common source of discouragement is other people. In 2:3, Haggai uses a rhetorical question to rebuke the older folks. "Who is left among you that saw this house in her first glory? and how do ye see it now? is it not in your eyes in comparison of it as nothing?" A companion passage, Ezra 3:12, tells us the rest of the story. "But many of the priests and Levites and chief of the fathers, who were ancient men, that had seen the first house, when the foundation of this house was laid before their eyes, wept with a loud voice; and many shouted aloud for joy." When the temple foundation was finished, some people shouted for joy, but others cried loudly because of the appearance of the new temple. They didn't like it. They remembered the incredible beauty of Solomon's temple and shed tears of disappointment. Their tearful, disparaging attitude may have been the cause of the Israelites' discouragement. Though the older folks' attitude was childish and unreasonable, the Devil used their whining and crying to discourage God's people.

You offer your bright idea to spruce up the yard by planting Venus flytraps in pots painted like your favorite NASCAR racers . . . but your wife responds with an ugly look. At church, a naysayer opposes your new building program with encouraging words like, "We can't afford it. We'll never fill up that building," or "We should have used my cousin for the builder." I doubt if church members stay up Saturday night composing mean things to say on Sunday, but they often speak before thinking, spewing negative comments that discourage all within hearing.

Henry Ford said the ability to encourage others is one of life's finest traits. As a young man, he made a drawing of his newly built engine and showed it to several people who laughed. Then he had dinner with Thomas Edison, also showing him the drawing. Edison studied it for awhile, banged his fist on the table and shouted, "Young man, that's the thing. You have it!"

Ford said later, "The thump of that fist on the table was worth worlds to me."

Haggai presented a four-point plan to conquer discouragement. As I open up this plan, you will see that the problem was not the circumstances but the way the people looked at their circumstances. Haggai essentially says, "Change the way you look at circumstances." You cannot change your circumstances. They are ordered by a sovereign, loving God. But you can change the way you look at them. Rather than focusing on the disappointment, the broken thing, the failure, or the fear, you must learn to look to God. Change your outlook to chase away discouragement.

Victory over Discouragement

To have victory over discouragement, Haggai challenges us to look at God, the past, the timing, and the final score.

1. Look at God (Hag. 2:4).

Three times in verse 4, Haggai used the phrase "saith the LORD." The word *LORD* is written in all capital letters in the KJV, so in Hebrew it is the name Jehovah. To the Jews, Jehovah was the most personal, sacred name of God. Haggai encouraged the people to focus on their personal God.

Your Omnipresent God Encourages

When Haggai reported God's words, "Work, for I am with you" (2:4), he was reminding the people that God is omnipresent. Since God is everywhere, He is always with you when you need Him. When discouragement strikes, God is there (Ps. 139:7–10). That may happen on Sunday morning when lightning and thunder tell you a storm is about to threaten your church attendance. It may come in the middle of the night when you awake to worry about the future, or when you are alone and demons unleash all their power to tempt you to sin.

Or when a church member informs you his needs can be met more effectively by a different pastor. Or when you sit with your wife in the doctor's office and hear those heart-stopping words, "It may be cancer." I speak from experience.

We had just started a revival meeting in a small church in Ohio. For several weeks, Claudia had struggled with abdominal pain. A local doctor ordered an immediate ultrasound. The next morning we sat in his office. "Sir, there is 50–50 possibility your wife has the most deadly cancer common to women." We canceled that meeting, hooked up our trailer, loaded our three kids into the truck, and drove south to a hospital near Claudia's parents.

We did not tell our children the seriousness of the illness, so they were as cheerful as usual on the trip. But Claudia and I traveled in a trance. The weather was beautiful, the mountain scenery lovely, but our thoughts were on the future. We stopped for a break at our favorite rest stop on the Tennessee border. Watching the children frolic in the grass, we had a matter-of-fact discussion about my raising three children without their mother. Though scared and sad, we had peace. God was giving us grace to make it through that day.

The next few weeks held doctor visits, tests, and surgery. The tests did not clearly reveal if the mass was cancer, so we would not know until the surgery. Each day we wondered, but each day we survived as God continued to supply daily strength. On the surgery day, Claudia's dad and I waited in her hospital room as the doctor worked. I remembered past wonderful times waiting in the hospital during the births of our children. This was not the same. I was now waiting to hear if my wife was healthy or dying with cancer. My survival mode switched from one-day-at-a-time to one-minute-at-a-time. God can handle that too.

The telephone rang, and the news was good. It was not cancer.

The operation was successful and my wife recovered quickly. I am thankful our anxiety level remained low during the entire medical adventure. We had both sensed God's presence as we sat in the doctor's office, during the long trip to the hospital, while the surgery was taking place, and during Claudia's recovery. Our omnipresent God was with us, just as He is with you right now.

A Sunday school teacher asked her class this question, "Why is there but one God?" One bright student replied, "Because God is in every place, and there is no room for anyone else."

Your Sovereign God Encourages

In verse 2:8 Haggai preached, "The silver is mine, and the gold is mine, saith the Lord." Before he died, King David had amassed millions in gold, silver, and precious stones for Solomon's temple. Now the economy was an inflationary mess. Where would they get the money to build a temple like Solomon's? Haggai reminded them that the God Who provided for Solomon's temple was still alive. He is the sovereign king of circumstances.

Your God knows all about you. According to Paul, He is working in your life to help you become like Christ (Rom. 8:29). Trials are a necessary tool to make you like the Savior. Since God is only good, He will never send a bad thing into the life of His child (Ps. 145:9). He cannot act contrary to His nature. He sends custom-designed trials to help you know Him better, to aid you in being conformed to the image of His Son. Learn to look at even potentially discouraging circumstances as tools in the hand of God. He makes no mistakes.

What is your trial today? Do you think God has allowed it because He is cruel, unloving, or has forgotten you? No. He works in love to break down your pride, to encourage you to die to self, to open the door to complete God-dependence. Stop questioning His sovereign plans and methods. Look through the trial at an omnipresent God, Who does not ask you to suffer alone. Focus on your sovereign God, Who sends each trial for His holy purpose and your growth in grace. Look at God.

2. Look at the past (Hag. 2:5).

Haggai reminded the Jews of their forefathers' victory in the past, "According to the word that I covenanted with you when ye came out of Egypt, so my spirit remains among you: fear ye not" (2:5). God had delivered them from Egyptian bondage. He was still alive to deliver them from fear and discouragement. Do you need courage in the midst of trying circumstances? Remember God's goodness in your past. The same God Who delivered you in the past is able to deliver you today.

The prophet spoke of their deliverance. That should be your starting point when viewing the past. The most glorious deliverance God provides is salvation from hell. Think about the day you chose to receive Jesus as Savior. On that day you obtained freedom from the bondage and pain of hell. Because of one supernatural moment of repentance and faith, God guaranteed you eternal life in heaven. Since God can deliver a soul from hell in a moment, don't you believe He can give you grace to survive your present day of darkness?

What if God has chosen pain, rejection, and death to be your lot in life, like past martyrs for the faith? What if that disease you have is His tool to usher you home to Him? What if the failure you face is ordained by the sovereign One to quench pride, which keeps you from enjoying untold blessings? Though no one welcomes pain, heartbreak, or failure, if you are God's child, His will is always kind, loving, and for your good. If you allow any circumstance to rob you of courage, you are forgetting you are on His side and headed for the glories of heaven. Remember your day of deliverance from eternal death.

Next, recall past trials from which God provided relief. Are you facing a financial trial? Remember similar crunches of the past and how God took care of you in them. Is it a medical adventure? Recall similar medical trials and trust the same Great Physician to see you through. Are you struggling in your marriage or concerned about your children? Remember past evidences of God's everlasting and longsuffering love. Remember when God gave you the wisdom you sorely needed.

The psalmist David often recalled past victories to encourage himself in present battles. In Psalm 18, David recalled deliverance from Saul and other enemies and was encouraged that "so shall I be saved from my enemies" (18:3). In Psalm 23, as David looked toward his approaching valley of the shadow of death, he rejoiced that just as God had led him to green pastures and still waters throughout life, He would surely deliver him from the dark shadow of earth's final enemy. Remember the past and be encouraged in the present.

One summer we pulled our trailer onto the grounds of a youth camp. We parked beside the dining hall and plugged our electric cord into a wall outlet. Soon we discovered that we did not have adequate electricity for our large trailer.

A kind man offered to help. I handed him the electric plug connected to the end of our long extension cord. He disappeared into the dining hall basement and in a few magic moments accidentally wired our 110-volt trailer into 220 volts of electricity. Oops. All the appliances in our trailer instantly went home to be with the Lord—television, VCR, stereo, microwave, and over-priced RV refrigerator. This was a perfect time to succumb to my Italian heritage and lose my temper.

However, Claudia later said that I maintained an unusual amount of self-control during the trial. How? I counted to ten, then twenty, then one hundred. While counting, I remembered God's care for us in the past. I recalled how I had pulled our trailer into a mud-hole in Tennessee and God sent someone to pull us out. I remembered the time we broke a trailer spring in

Ohio, and a stranger spent a day repairing it for free. I remembered that we survived our first winter in evangelism in New England's frigid cold and snow—living in a poorly insulated RV. I remembered the blown tire on the Chicago freeway and the time we lost control of our rig on I-95 in Maryland and survived. I chuckled as I recalled the time we were pulling our trailer down a Georgia highway. I suddenly saw a stray wheel rolling past the front left side of the truck. It looked like one of our six trailer wheels. It was! Apparently I had failed to tighten the lug nuts.

God took care of us in each of those trailer trials. Surely He would take care of this one.

I encouraged myself in the present by recalling God's provision in the past. God helped us through that trailer trial. When we left two weeks later, the appliances had been resurrected (hallelujah!) and many teenagers had come to the Savior. The same God Who has taken care of you in the past can deliver you in the present. To conquer discouragement, look at the past.

3. Look at the timing (Hag. 2:6).

The prophet reminds his hearers that "it is a little while" before God prepares the earth for end-time events, including the building of another temple. Verses 6–9 prophesy that in a little while God will shake the heavens and the earth in tribulation judgment (Rev. 6–16). Christ, the "desire of all nations," will return in victory, and He will reign on the throne of another temple, here called the "latter house." Since no one but God knows the exact time of Christ's return, the phrase "a little while" cannot represent an absolute number of days. It obviously means a short time. Our attitude toward Christ's return should be that He will return in a little while! Though a little while may be many years, your daily outlook should be this: Jesus may come today. It is the same with the timing of discouragement.

Discouragement must be viewed as temporary. You will get discouraged again and again before you go home. So will I. It may happen before you finish reading this book. Or when you, church planter, receive notice that you must move out of your present location and find a new one. Or when you, pastor, hear of covert efforts to get you to move on to another church. Or when your wife hears critical words about her husband. Or when you, faithful missionary, receive an unkind email from another missionary across the city. It may happen when you least expect it. But it will happen. It will come. Now is the time to permanently etch this in your memory: discouragement is to be "a little while." It is to be short.

If you allow discouragement to drag on, you may find yourself enjoying the special attention from others. You may begin to cherish their expressions of sympathy. You might even decline in your spirit from discouragement to self-pity, a martyr complex, or even full-blown depression. It is possible to worry and depress yourself into a hospital mental ward. If that happens to someone you know, do not judge him. Never say, "I told you so." Sympathize with him and do what you can to nurse him back to mental and spiritual health. But decide right now that that is not God's will for you. You do not have to let discouragement lead to despair. The moment you know you are in the hole of discouragement, get alone with God and talk to Him. If necessary, seek counsel. Bearing one another's burdens includes helping each other through discouraging times. When I pastored, several times I mentioned my pain of discouragement to the congregation during Wednesday night prayer time. Before the night was over, God had used fellow believers to speak words of encouragement. I headed home rejoicing that He is only good.

Someone said, "It is not a sin to fall into the hole of discouragement, but it is sinful to pick up a shovel and proceed to bury yourself." I agree. Discouragement is to be temporary. Ask God for help to work on the problem. Read Haggai 2, get help from a ministry friend, and climb out of the hole of despair.

4. Look at the final score (2:6–9).

As I mentioned, verses 6–9 prophesy the future temple that the Jews will enjoy in fulfillment of God's covenant promises. Though throughout history enemies have oppressed and tried to annihilate God's people, the Jews are on His winning side. My view of eschatology tells me that in fulfillment of God's promises to Israel, Christ will rule for a thousand years in a rebuilt temple in Jerusalem (Rev. 20:1–6). The Jews did not understand the prophetic implications then, but they could surely agree that they were on God's victory side.

Though Haggai was speaking to the Jews, his words of encouragement apply to all who are born again, Jew and Gentile. Every believer in Jesus will in some way enjoy the blessings of the millennium. Satan will eventually be cast alive into the lake of fire to be punished forever (Rev. 20:10). Though the evil one is alive and well today, he will be the ultimate loser, forever. The outcome in the battle between the Devil and God will be this: God wins, Satan loses. No matter how much the Evil One works to discourage you, you are on the winning side!

Evil men do wax worse and worse. Satan does continue to rage and plot and attack and torment. But Paul said in Romans 8:18 that "the sufferings of this present time are not worthy to be compared with the glory which shall be revealed in us." You are on the winning side. Reject discouragement. Look at God, look at the past, look at the timing, look at the final score. Take courage . . . and press on.

Living Chapter 4

1. True or false? It is God's will for the believer to live in constant fear.

2. Memorize 2 Timothy 1:7—"For God hath not given us the spirit of fear; but of power, and of love, and of a sound mind."

3. List specific ways God has met your needs in the past.

4. List people who have encouraged you over the years.

5. Think of someone else who needs to be encouraged and do something to encourage him or her.

6. Review the definition of *success* in chapter 2.

PRESS *ON!* 5

. . . IN SPITE OF TEMPTATION

I often laugh at Satan, and there is nothing that makes him so angry as when I attack him to his face and tell him that through God I am more than a match for him. (Charles H. Spurgeon)

Blessed is the man that endureth temptation: for when he is tried, he shall receive the crown of life, which the Lord hath promised to them that love him. (James 1:12)

When I was a child, my mom often said, "David, don't hate anything but sin or anyone but the Devil!" That's good counsel. I do hate the Devil. Temptation runs a close second. Twenty-four hours a day, every day, Satan pursues God's children, especially His full-time servants. Seneca said, "O that a hand would come down from heaven and deliver me from my besetting sin!"

When I was in my twenties, I noted older men in ministry and wondered if the temptations of my flesh would get weaker as I aged. Now that I am approaching sixty, I can say from experience that they do not. I am more aware of Satan's methods, more sensitive to sin, and more determined to please God. But my flesh is still alive and irritatingly healthy. Temptations are powerful, constantly lurking, waiting to take me (and you) out of the ministry. Since the flesh does not improve during this pilgrim journey, we all must always be on guard.

In our depravity, we tend to imitate Israel's cycle of behavior found in the book of Judges: sin, confession, victory, and return to sin. We blame our sin on God, our spouses, our culture, our bloodlines, our circumstances, and the Devil. Like the nation of Israel, after we sin, we cry out to God, enjoy His forgiveness, press on in victory for a while, and then stumble again in the face of constant, nagging temptation. Someone aptly said, "At birth we have a wedding. We are wedded to temptation and Satan proclaims, 'til death do us part.'"

Satan wants to take you down. He knows he is a defeated foe. He knows he will eventually be tormented in the lake of fire (Rev. 20:10). He knows that if you are truly born again he cannot get your soul, for you are held securely by God's hand, protected by the blood of Christ (John 10:27–29). The Evil One therefore works hard to destroy your most valuable earthly asset—your public testimony.

Lose your testimony, lose your credibility. Lose your testimony, and your commendable traits will be almost worthless. Your ability to preach, skill in administration, intellectual prowess, esteem among peers, impressive degrees and awards, even your track record of accomplishments, will be negated. Since Satan knows this, he cackles with joy when a servant of God chooses to sin away his testimony. He is working at this moment to plot, scheme, scam, and stumble you into sin.

Since God is all-powerful, why does He allow temptation to continue? Though we cannot fully understand the mind and purposes of God, at least two reasons He allows temptation are to try your loyalty and to strengthen your weakness.

To Try Your Loyalty

You may talk about being loyal to God, appear to be loyal to God, and even be convinced that you are loyal to God. But you actually prove your loyalty when you conquer temptation.

Abraham appeared to be loyal to God, and God gave him the opportunity to prove it. In obedience to God's command, he trekked up the mountain in the land of Moriah (Gen. 22:2) and prepared to offer his son Isaac as a sacrifice. When he lifted up the knife to kill him, the angel of the Lord appeared and said, "Lay not thine hand upon the lad, neither do thou any thing unto him: for now I know that thou fearest God, seeing thou hast not withheld thy son, thine only son from me" (Gen. 22:12). God was trying his loyalty. Abraham was tempted to disobey God and spare Isaac. But he passed the test. He proved that he loved God more than he loved his son, more than he loved his present happiness, more than he loved himself.

God places you in the crucible of difficult choices so that you can choose God instead of the world. First John 2:15 says, "If any man love the world, the love of the Father is not in him." He may allow a teenager to be tempted to sin with evil companions; but as he rejects the temptation, he proves his loyalty to God. God may allow a full-time servant like you to be tempted to immorality. But as you reject that sin, you prove your loyalty to God. Each temptation leaves you better or worse—worse if you yield, better if you have victory and display your loyalty to your Redeemer. God may be trying your loyalty right now. How are you responding? How will you respond? Whom do you really love? To whom will you be loyal?

To Reveal and Strengthen Weakness

God may allow you to be tempted to strengthen a weakness. Just as weightlifting shows us our physical weaknesses and strengthens physical muscles through stressing and stretching, temptation can reveal areas of spiritual weakness and provide ways to build spiritual muscles. Someone said that talent is formed in solitude and character in the storms of life. God may allow temptation to show you how much work He needs to do in you.

When Israel wandered in the wilderness, tired and discouraged by the slowness of travel and the impatience of Moses, God said, "And thou shalt remember all the way which the LORD thy God led thee these forty years in the wilderness, to humble thee, and to prove thee, to know what was in thine heart, whether thou wouldest keep his commandments, or no" (Deut. 8:2). God allowed His people to be tested to try their loyalties, to bring out hidden sinfulness, pride, and self-sufficiency.

God gave Paul a "thorn in the flesh, the messenger of Satan to buffet me, lest I should be exalted above measure" (2 Cor. 12:7). We are not told the nature of the thorn. Possibly it was a physical affliction, or maybe it was a besetting temptation he battled until death. Whatever it was, Paul three times asked God to remove the affliction. God's answer was "My grace is sufficient for thee: for my strength is made perfect in weakness" (2 Cor. 12:9). That is an encouraging, liberating statement! God says that your weakness can be the manifestation of His strength, His power, His grace. God may allow you to endure temptation to remind you that He is your ultimate source of victory. Temptation does not have to become a source of failure. Instead, it can remind you to totally depend on God.

> The Lord has more need of our weakness than of our strength: our strength is often His rival; our weakness, His servant, drawing on His resources and showing forth His glory. Man's extremity is God's opportunity; man's security is Satan's opportunity. God's way is not to take His children out of trial but to give them strength to bear up against it.[1]

1. Jamieson-Faucett Brown Commentary. PowerBible CD 5.6.

Are you struggling right now with a particularly tough and persistent temptation? You may be on the verge of enjoying God's grace like never before. God allows you to be tempted to reveal and strengthen your weaknesses.

Winning over Temptation

As long as you live, temptation lives with you. It cannot be eliminated. But you can have more victory than defeat. Just as Satan labors to cause you to stumble, the Lord Jesus is interceding for you. As your sympathetic high priest (Heb. 8:1), Jesus prays continuously that you will understand who Satan is, recognize his evil methods (Eph. 6:11), and do what is necessary to conquer sin. He not only will give you the means to conquer but He also promises rewards when you endure. "Blessed is the man that endureth temptation: for when he is tried, he shall receive the crown of life, which the Lord hath promised to them that love him" (James 1:12). That is grace added to grace!

Temptation attacks you on three fronts: your own hearts (Jer. 17:9; James 1:13–15), the world (1 John 2:16), and Satan and his demons (1 Pet. 5:8, Eph. 6:12). A military strategist said, "Knowing your enemy is your first step to victory." To help you find your way to constant victory, let's examine Satan's character, his methods, and his defeat.

Satan's Character—Not Mr. Nice Guy

Satan is a hateful, diligent, lying tempter. Though he knows that God will one day cast him into the lake of fire (Rev. 20:10), he audaciously tempted Jesus in the wilderness (Matt. 4:1–3). He filled the hearts of Ananias and Sapphira to lie to the Holy Ghost (Acts 5). When Paul, Timothy, and Silvanus wanted to visit the saints in Thessalonica, hindered them (1 Thess. 2:18). Satan is an evil, malicious demon who never gives up on you.

He Is Hateful

As hatred personified, Satan hates everything except himself. Revelation 12 calls Satan the great Dragon, the old serpent, and the Devil, who deceives the whole world. The chapter trumpets a warning to the inhabitants of the earth that "the devil is come down unto you, having great wrath, because he knoweth that he hath but a short time" (Rev. 12:12). Satan's hatred makes him dangerously persistent in his attempt to lead you into evil. He never gives you a break.

Satan never says, "I see that Pastor So-and-So had a hard week. A family left the church because 'they were not being fed.' One of his deacons was caught in an adulterous affair—with my help, of course. He is tired from a late night hospital visit. He is having difficulties with one of his children. Since he's going through a tough time, I think I will let up on him. I will have compassion and leave him alone for a few days." The great Dragon never extends mercy like that. The fact is that he does just the opposite. When he sees you down, he turns up the fire of temptation. Since he knows your besetting sin, he sends skillful, hateful demons that specialize in your weakness.

Picture yourself lying in the middle of a busy street. The automobile that has knocked you down speeds away as you cry out in pain. A passerby strolls over, sneers at you, and with all his strength kicks you in your aching stomach, your bruised back, your broken legs, and finally your bleeding head.

"Inhuman behavior!" you protest. "How could anyone be so rotten, so insensitive, so hateful?" Such is the heart of Satan. He is not human. He is a fallen, evil angel who laughs when you are down, attacks when you are discouraged, and labors untiringly to lead you into temptation. He is capable of more evil than you can imagine. He is one bad, hateful tempter.

He Is Diligent

Satan never tires. He is always working, consistently diligent, allowing nothing to hinder his agenda to trip you up. Peter warns, "Be sober, be vigilant; because your adversary the devil, as a roaring lion, walketh about, seeking whom he may devour" (1 Pet. 5:8). You are exhorted to be vigilant (stay awake, watch) because Satan is equally vigilant. He and his demons are walking about the earth, actively working twenty-four hours a day to taunt, tempt, and deceive.

The Bible never states or even suggests that Satan needs to rest. Though horribly evil, he is still a fallen angel with supernatural strength. Though not wise, since true wisdom is in knowing and loving God, he is clever and creative. He noted the greed of Judas and tempted him to betray Christ for a bit of silver. When he sees you resisting the sin of lust, he may turn his efforts to pride. If he cannot get you to covet, he dangles complacency before you. If you refuse to get discouraged, he may lead you into presumption. As you avoid doctrinal error, he may tempt you with dead formalism.

Just as the sun is always shining somewhere on earth, the prince of darkness with his principalities and powers of evil is always awake—watching, planning, and laboring— to thwart God's kingdom by leading a saint like you into sin. Be always on guard, because the diligent Devil is always on the job.

He Is a Liar

According to John 8:44, Satan is the father of lies. Though he has a massive arsenal of weapons, lying is his most effective tool. He tells you that no one else struggles with your unique temptation (1 Pet. 5:9). He lies. He tries to convince you that there is no way to escape (1 Cor. 10:13). He lies. He argues that you must sin, that you deserve to sin because of the behavior of someone such as your wife, your children, or your church members (1 Thess. 4:7). He lies. He wants you to believe that God has forgotten or forsaken you or that He is depriving you of a deserved pleasure (Jer. 31:3; Rom. 8:28). He lies.

Satan whispers that you are destined to sin because of your upbringing, "Since your relative had a temper, succumbed to lust, committed suicide—so must you!" He lies. You have the Holy Spirit living within you, and His power is infinitely greater than the influence of background or genes (1 John 4:4). If you blame your background or upbringing for your sin, you are blaming an omnipotent God, Who is more powerful than your past. Satan is a liar. Stop listening to him and ask for wisdom to detect his lies.

Satan's Methods—His Times and Tools

His Times of Attack

The Devil never announces his intention to hound you. He comes when you are tired, discouraged, angry, worried, even when you are spiritually refreshed. You can prepare for victory by learning to identify his seasons of battle.

At the time of conviction. Do you remember Satan's earliest onslaught? The Holy Spirit stirred your conscience to convince you of your need for Christ. The Devil was energized. He worked with hate-filled enthusiasm to convince you that your good works, your baptism, or your church membership would suffice for salvation. "You have plenty of time to repent and trust Christ," sneered Satan. But you chose to turn from sin and received the Savior.

At the time of salvation. Before you received Christ, you were a slave to darkness. But as a new believer you became a special target for the Devil's ire. "You did not sincerely repent!" demons scream. "Your faith will not last. You are too weak to live the

Christian life. Your past sins are too terrible to be forgiven." Recall the hinderer's efforts during the early days of your salvation and be sensitive to newly born ones under your care. Warn them of the accuser's efforts to confuse and discourage. Teach, nourish, and be patient.

At times of idleness. If you do not have a plan for your day, the Devil will make one for you. King David should have been leading his men in battle, but he sat alone, idle on his rooftop, and soon sinned with Bathsheba. Though rest and recreation can be a good stewardship of time and energy, idleness is a prime time for demonic assaults. Be careful when on vacation. Be on guard during times of leisure. Watch diligently when surfing the Internet, viewing the television, or even strolling through the mall. Servants of God have stumbled into sin when at leisure.

At times of low resources. After Christ had fasted for forty days, Satan tempted Him (Matt. 4:1–12). Temptation is stirred by desire (James 1:14), so the greater the desire, the greater the temptation. Adam was tempted by a bit of fruit, but Jesus abstained from all food for forty days. Jesus' sore temptation came when He was hungry and physically weak.

Be aware when your resources are low. Satan swings into action when he sees you sick, tired, hungry, or financially troubled. He delights to see your relationship with your wife in crisis. He will attack when you feel like a failure or allow yourself to court a bitter spirit. If you neglect your Bible, abandon prayer, or excuse sin, your spiritual resources will be low. Satan will take advantage of you.

At times of spiritual refreshing. Again, Elijah is our teacher. He appeared to be a great spiritual success that night on Mt. Carmel. His prayer opened the heavens and God responded. But the next morning he made a cowardly dash for the desert and asked God to take his life (1 Kings 19:4). It appears that Satan took advantage of spiritual pride. A fall ensued.

Rejoice in times of spiritual victory! But stay on guard. Expect Satan to sneak up on you when you are spiritually energized. "Wherefore let him that thinketh he standeth take heed lest he fall" (1 Cor. 10:12).

At times of service. When you serve God, the Devil is angry. You are praying, you are preaching, you are counseling, you are studying—and Satan is fuming. He will hinder you.

I recall several ministry opportunities when this happened. Comfortably seated in the living room of a needy soul, with my Bible open, carefully explaining the way of salvation, I began to feel drowsy! How could that happen? I was engaged in the life-changing, soul-rescuing activity of sharing the truth! I struggled to make my words clear and to stay focused. Why such a battle? The answer is simple. The Devil hates you when you do more than just talk about evangelism, prayer, or loving others. When you actually do something for God, Satan attacks. Watch therefore and be on guard.

His Tools of Temptation

Satan, a fallen angel, is the prince of darkness with power to deceive the whole world. He has a formidable armory of tools. In 2 Corinthians 2:11, Paul warns, "Lest Satan should get an advantage of us: for we are not ignorant of his devices [evil plans and purposes]." Among others, his weapons of destruction include deception, envy, bitterness, ambition, covetousness, discouragement, sexual lust, and pride.

How does Satan use his tools against you? What methods does he use to scam you into yielding to temptation? Here are three of his most powerful and effective methods. Take note and use your knowledge as a tool to defeat him.

Bait and hook. As a youngster growing up in Tennessee, I loved to fish for catfish in a nearby lake. It didn't require fancy equipment or expensive bait. My Sears & Roebuck rod and reel, a few hooks, a baloney sandwich with mustard and a pickle, and a tin of biscuit dough were all I needed for a day of fun. (In the hands of my mom, the biscuit dough could have been gloriously transformed into succulent southern blackberry jam holders, but at the lake it was tempting bait for hungry catfish.)

On a typical afternoon fishing expedition, I would lie on shore in the sun, slipping peacefully into a heat-induced nap, only to be awakened by a sharp tug on my line. Apparently, a bottom-feeding catfish smelled the delectable dough, chomped down on his lunch, and was snared by the hook. The old bait-and-hook ploy worked. The bait looked good and smelled good, but it was not good. It concealed the hook. Satan used the same tool when he promised Eve that if she'd eat the forbidden fruit she would "not surely die . . . but be as gods, knowing good and evil" (Gen. 3:4–5). Eve fell for it. And the human race followed.

Just as God called Peter and Andrew to be fishers of men, Satan actively fishes for God's men. The bait that tempts you to sin deceptively hides the barbed hook of sin's consequences—guilt, loss of peace, power, joy, God's blessing—sometimes even loss of life (1 John 5:16). He dangles the bait of social drinking but conceals the hook of alcoholism. He may lure you with the bait of sexual pleasure while hiding the hook of slavery to pornography. That offer to seek greener grass in ministry may be concealing the hook of leaving the present, though difficult, will of God.

Be on guard against this subtle, evil method. The Devil's bait never looks distasteful. It always looks delicious, but one bite of his delights may deliver a mouthful of putrid globs of diseased sin, complete with consequences that last for years.

"A little sin won't hurt." Satan will trick you into viewing sin through his personal, perverted telescope. He subtly turns it around. Looking through the wrong end, sin appears small.

Yet Galatians 5:9 warns, "A little leaven leaveneth the whole lump." What confidence would you have in a doctor who analyzed your medical tests and concluded, "Well, sir, we did find some cancer cells, but they are tiny. They may be deadly, but since they are so small, we will just ignore them"? Imagine that your wife, while stirring cake batter, watches a cockroach crawl up the side of the bowl and into the batter. Calmly stirring, she quips, "It's only a small bug. Probably a good source of protein. The family will think I added a few crunchy nuts."

The massive rope that secures an ocean liner to the dock may be twenty-four inches in diameter. If you look closer, you'll see that it is made up of numerous small strands of cord wrapped together to form one powerful rope. Small sins will eventually become one large cable. One evil suggestion, one illicit thought, and one ungodly idea after another will eventually be twisted into a strong rope of sin that binds.

No sin must be considered small. All ill winds of sin blow contrary to the perfect holiness of God. You must view any sin as the sin that cost the death of Christ. Did your sin today inspire the Romans to crucify Him? Is the sin that Satan tells you is insignificant designed to lead you to greater sin and irreversible consequences? Satan lies when he says, "A little sin won't hurt."

"Repent tomorrow." The Bible never encourages delayed repentance. Satan does. When he detects a desire for repentance, he reminds you that sin feels good. Demons may whisper, "Wait until tomorrow to repent. Enjoy the pleasure one more day. Your good God will be as merciful tomorrow as today."

Consider two sobering problems of putting off repentance. First, you are living under the wrath of a holy God. Holiness demands that He punish sin. The lost man who puts off repentance and faith in Christ will eventually be cast into hell. The believer who delays repentance risks the loss of God's longsuffering. Because "whom the Lord loveth, he chasteneth" (Heb. 12:6), you risk experiencing the rod of God. His chastening rod is designed to instruct and help you avoid further sin, but it still hurts.

Second, the longer you delay repentance, the harder it may be to repent. A broken bone is easier set if taken care of immediately. Cancer is more easily cured if caught in an early stage. Are you dabbling with sin right now? Have you taken the deceiver's bait? Are you now beginning to feel the sharp barb of the hook? Stop the sin. Repent right now (1 John 1). It is the Devil, who hates you, who says, "Tomorrow is the time to repent."

A group of college students were ice skating on a partially frozen lake. The authorities arrived, tested the ice, and warned that the ice was getting dangerously thin. All the students got off the ice except one young man. As he enthusiastically took off for one more lap, he proclaimed, "Just one more time around!" When he reached the halfway point of the circular track, the ice broke. He fell into the water and drowned.

The wages of sin are always death. They will certainly be the death of personal peace and joy. They may also be the death of a marriage, a ministry, or God's blessing. They may even be physical death. Don't delay repentance.

His Defeat—You Can Win

Though Satan is ruthless, God is more powerful. With God's help, you can resist the Devil, expect him to flee (James 4:7), and live in victory. Think about the sin that so easily besets you—the sin that keeps you off balance, discouraged, and feeling guilty. Perhaps you have struggled with it for years. Perhaps because of that sin, you are on the verge of destroying your marriage, your ministry, or your public testimony.

Whatever that sin is, God is able to deliver you! There is no magical, instant solution. Being conformed to the image of Christ, which is Christian growth, is not instantaneous. It is a process. Progressive sanctification (the lifetime process of becoming like Christ) takes time. Resisting Satan is a daily, often moment-by-moment battle. But it is a battle that you can win. Though many lengthy books have been written about temptation, I offer you a simple four-pronged plan of attack. May God use it to help you enjoy moral freedom and victory.

Thank God for the Temptation

First Thessalonians 5:18 says, "In every thing give thanks." Giving thanks for every temptation is the first step to victory. A grateful heart, thankful for all things in the will of God, is a powerful tool. The Devil suggested to Eve that God was robbing her of the privilege of being like Him. Eve believed his lie and yielded to temptation. If Satan can convince you that God is robbing you of something good, you may doubt His love.

Satan will taunt, "God doesn't really love you, or He would let you indulge your pet sin. Your desire is not that bad. The unsaved world enjoys it. God is depriving you of needed pleasure because He does not love you."

Rather than listen to the Devil's lie, pray immediately and thank God that He is only good: "Dear God, thank You for allowing this temptation. I know that You are only good, and that this temptation is given for my good and Your glory. I know You have provided a way to escape. Help me to find it and take it. Thank You that I have an opportunity to enjoy Your love and experience Your power through this temptation."

Don't allow yourself to question God's love. Refuse to believe Satan's lie that God is depriving you of deserved pleasure. If you allow the Devil access to your mind and doubt God, he will continue his lies and deceive you into sin.

Assume Responsibility for Your Sin

You will never conquer sin until you admit that it is sin, that it is your sin, and that it is your responsibility. When God confronted Adam in the Garden of Eden, Adam blamed Eve for his sin. "And the man said, The woman whom thou gavest to be with me, she gave me of the tree, and I did eat" (Gen. 3:12). Most of us are quick to blame someone else for our sin.

It is a mistake to blame your sin on your forefathers. Exodus 20:5 speaks of "God, visiting the iniquity of the fathers upon the children unto the third and fourth generation of them that hate me," but the next verse says, "shewing mercy unto thousands of them that love me, and keep my commandments." You may have inherited sinful tendencies sown by your forefathers, but you do not have to yield. You can choose to keep God's commandments. He offers mercy to any who choose to keep His commandments.

Though the smell of alcohol may tempt you, you must choose to stay away. Your dad may have had a violent temper, but that is not an excuse for your sin. One of your blood relatives may have been lazy, covetous, adulterous, or suicidal. But as a believer, you have the Holy Spirit living within you (1 Cor. 6:19–20). The fruit of the Spirit includes all you need to conquer any sin, if you choose. "But the fruit of the Spirit is love, joy, peace, longsuffering, gentleness, goodness, faith, meekness, temperance: against such there is no law" (Gal. 5:22–23). When you say, "I have to yield to greed because my parents were greedy," you deny the power of the Holy Spirit.

Stop blaming others (including the Devil) for your sin. The moment you take full responsibility for your sin, you deal a blow to Satan's demonic forces. When you encourage yourself by saying, "If I commit this sin, it is my own fault," you are on the road to victory.

Claim the Victory of the Cross

When Jesus died on the cross, He did more than satisfy the

penalty that God required. His victory over death provided potential victory over temptation. "Who gave himself for our sins, that he might deliver us from this present evil world, according to the will of God and our Father" (Gal. 1:4). When faced with temptation, you must claim the victory of the cross.

Adam fell prey to temptation and gave in to the flesh. As a result, all have sinned. All men, including believers, will battle the flesh until "death us do part." In Adam, you are doomed to sin and keep on sinning, but in Christ, the second Adam, Who permanently disabled Satan on the cross, you can win over sin!

At least a hundred times, Paul says that as a believer, you are "in Christ."

> There is therefore now no condemnation to them which are in Christ Jesus. (Rom. 8:1)
>
> So we . . . are one body in Christ. (Rom. 12:5)
>
> Paul an apostle . . . to the saints . . . and to the faithful in Christ Jesus. (Eph. 1:1)

Being in Christ, you share all that He owns and all that He has accomplished. On the cross, Jesus Christ not only dealt the blow of eternal death to Satan but also provided potential victory over all your temptations. The key concept is found in Romans 6.

> What shall we say then? Shall we continue in sin, that grace may abound? God forbid. How shall we, that are dead to sin, live any longer therein? Know ye not, that so many of us as were baptized into Jesus Christ were baptized into his death? Therefore we are buried with him by baptism into death: that like as Christ was raised up from the dead by the glory of the Father, even so we also should walk in newness of life. For if we have been planted together in the

> likeness of his death, we shall be also in the likeness of his resurrection: knowing this, that our old man is crucified with him, that the body of sin might be destroyed, that henceforth we should not serve sin. For he that is dead is freed from sin. (vv. 1–7)

Though you were not physically present, as a believer "in Christ" you died with Jesus on the cross, which means that His victory over Satan is also yours. His power in being raised from the dead is yours too. You have a theological right to say to Satan when he tempts, "My tendency to sin died with Jesus on the cross. I no longer have to obey you, Satan, for in Christ I have already been delivered from this temptation. I now claim the victory of the cross!"

Consider Romans 6:1–7 to be your Magna Carta of victory. When King John signed that document on June 15, 1215, it became the basis of English rights. Romans 6 is your legal document (guaranteed by the highest authority), stating that because of the cross of Jesus Christ all who are "in Christ" can conquer the Devil.

Obviously, "dead to sin" does not mean dead to temptation. Passions are alive and the flesh is with you until death. However, being in Christ legally guarantees that you have within you the potential to conquer any temptation, put to death any sinful habit or tendency, and live daily in victory. "For as in Adam all die, even so in Christ shall all be made alive" (1 Cor. 15:22).

Before you received Christ, you naturally yielded to the impulses and desires of the flesh. You were still "in Adam," and your efforts to conquer evil were determined by your upbringing, your friends, man's philosophies, and your own sinful heart. In Jesus Christ, Who is your new nature through the new birth, you have the Holy Spirit to show you the way to escape.

I am encouraged in my daily battles by Hebrews 2:14: "Forasmuch then as the children are partakers of flesh and blood, he also himself likewise took part of the same; that through death he might destroy him that had the power of death, that is, the devil." The Greek word for destroy, *katargeo,* means "to do away with" and to "make of none effect." Christ's death and resurrection makes Satan's malicious barbs "of no effect." His attacks are real, but they do not have to affect you.

To claim the cross victory, cry out to God in the time of temptation: "Dear Father, thank You that Jesus Christ conquered Satan forever on the cross. I thank You that because Christ was crucified and raised from the dead, I too have crucified the flesh with its affections and lusts. Thank You that Satan's temptations are of no effect. Thank You that You provide wisdom to find the way of escape. Help me right now to take it. By faith, because of the cross, I believe that victory is mine."

Continuously Renew Your Mind

Satan's battleground of temptation is your mind. If the great Dragon's lies succeed in leading you to wrong thinking, those wrong thoughts may lead to wrong actions. Thus, God challenges you to "be not conformed to this world: but be ye transformed by the renewing of your mind" (Rom. 12:2). Simply clenching your fist and resisting evil may cause Satan to attack with renewed persistence and determination. Freedom can be yours by saying no to each temptation while constantly filling your mind with God's thoughts.

How do you renew your mind?

1. Live in the Word of God. Start each day in the Word, asking God to search, challenge, and strengthen you.

2. Labor to be a Spirit-filled Christian (Eph. 5:18) with your sin accounts up to date, immediately confessing any known sin (1 John 1:9) and asking God to put it under the blood of Christ.

3. Memorize and meditate on Scripture passages that relate directly to your sin struggles, such as Romans 6:1–7, 1 Corinthians 10:13, 1 John 4:4, and James 4:7.

4. Beware of morning attacks. The moment of awakening is a crucial time of each day. It is a time when Satan may attempt to sow seeds of anger, doubt, bitterness, lust, laziness, and so forth. When you wake up, immediately thank God for another day, thank Him that you have victory because of the cross, and give the day to Him. Immediately spend time in the Bible and prayer.

5. Obey the first promptings of the Holy Spirit. He will stir you when Satan tries to influence your mind. When wrong thoughts enter, promptly claim victory by praying something like "I reject these thoughts of Satan. I now have Christ living in me. He is only good and always holy. Jesus has provided my escape and I now take it." Switch topics on the Devil and consciously return to right thinking.

Years ago, I worked as an assistant for a professor who taught pulpit speech. My job included listening to and evaluating student preachers. One creative student preached his sermon on running the race of the Christian life. The characters on his metaphorical race track included Christian, the chief runner, who was constantly being pursued by an evil enemy. The evil enemy's first name was Tim. His last name was Tation. Tim Tation was a ruthless, persistent adversary who dogged the heels of Christian. Mr. Tation never slowed down, slacked off, or gave up. He was always there, waiting to overcome and stumble Christian on the racetrack of life.

Pause for a moment to thank God that in Christ you have all you need to outrun Tim Tation. Put on the whole armor of God, claim the cross, and win over temptation.

Living Chapter 5

1. List specific baits that Satan uses against you, including hooks he conceals.

2. Memorize Romans 6:1–7; 1 Corinthians 10:13; 1 John 4:4; 1 Peter 5:8; 1 Corinthians 15:57–58; and James 4:7.

3. Memorize Scriptures that relate to your personal besetting sin.

4. Become accountable to a friend who will occasionally ask you how you are doing in the temptation battle. Pray for one another.

5. Resolve to start each day by committing your thoughts to God.

PRESS *ON!*

. . . THROUGH LIFE'S INEVITABLE NEGATIVES

6

I have learned that success is to be measured not so much by the position that one has reached in life as by the obstacles which he has had to overcome while trying to succeed.
(Booker T. Washington)

Therefore I take pleasure in infirmities, in reproaches, in needs, in persecutions, in distresses, for Christ's sake. For when I am weak, then I am strong. (2 Cor. 12:10)

Since 1868 the Southwestern Company of Nashville, Tennessee, has helped college students finance their education by selling books. They market family-oriented educational reference books and software through a summer sales force of over three thousand students. Remember my story in chapter 2 about the friendly dog I met as a college book salesman? Southwestern was my employer.

Before Southwestern sent me into the hot summer to knock on doors ten hours a day, they trained me in a one-week sales school. It was one of the most valuable weeks of my life.

Skilled, enthusiastic trainers taught me how to knock on a stranger's door, how to introduce the product, how to handle objections, and best of all, how to survive the negatives. To sell books, you must survive many noes to eventually find one yes. At sales school we were instructed in how to handle the noes, but the real training took place in the field via experience. Someone astutely called a summer internship with Southwestern "a crash course in life."

Are you convinced that your life is in the hands of your sovereign God? If you are, you can survive life's negatives. I am not talking about a man-centered "Something good is going to happen to you" humanistic ideology. I speak of viewing life's trials, rejection, and negatives in the context of knowing God, Who is only, always good. Knowing how to handle negatives is the difference between a top salesman and a mediocre one, the difference between the church planter who survives the start-up pains and one who quits when the ministry gets tough. It's a characteristic of the pastor who presses on though carnal Christians oppose him. Learning to handle negatives will allow God to turn your bitters into His sweets. It is biblical. It is doable. And in ministry, it is essential.

Let me ask you a question. While on earth, was Jesus Christ a popular person? His chosen nation helped put Him on the cross (John 1:11). His disciples deserted Him at that cross (Matt. 26:56). One disciple doubted Him after He had risen from the dead (John 20:25). Yet in order to finish the work of His Father, Christ willingly faced rejection from His own nation, race, family, and disciples. How did He survive? In part, because He is God. But there is more.

In His humanity, Christ dealt with more negatives than positives. He grew physically tired. He tasted discouragement, disappointment, and loneliness. As your faithful High Priest, He faced every temptation you face (Heb. 4:15). He was often misunderstood and occasionally tempted to quit. But He endured, pressed on, and conquered. How? Christ knew how to view negatives as positives. He endured the trials and the cross to finish the work of redemption—and then enjoyed the results of the resurrection.

Normal Christian ministry involves loads of rejection. When Paul entered cities to preach truth and plant churches, he was not greeted by welcoming throngs who looked forward to being told they were lost and headed for hell. He was rejected, ridiculed, beaten, even tossed out of cities and stoned. Church planter, you will face more rejection than acceptance in the early years of a new church. You will not discover hoards of people eager to hear the whole truth. You will struggle with more noes than yeses in the beginning years. Learning to survive the noes is a key to your survival. I am sorry to tell you, but when your new church is established, the negatives will continue! The pastor of any size church will concur. The helpmeet of a pastor, evangelist, or missionary will also face constant negatives, intended by the Devil to cripple her effectiveness and rob her of joy. Since Satan hates the work of God's soldiers, opposition to righteous service is normal Christian living.

Ministry survivalists often talk to themselves. You may have said to yourself, "I am going to preach the truth this morning in spite of Mrs. Sourpuss snarling at me from her back-row pew."

- "I am not going to punch Mr. Whiner in the nose tonight when he tells me his latest gripe."
- "I will stay here as pastor for at least one more month/week/minute."
- "I will not accidentally trip and dump coffee on that woman who gossiped about my wife."

Talking to yourself can be helpful. After all, self always listens and rarely responds. (If self does start talking back, please seek professional help.) Regardless of your age or ministry experience, you must learn to talk to yourself (via the intercessory voice of the Holy Spirit). Let me suggest two things you can say to yourself that will help you, by God's grace, turn your negatives to His positives. They are (1) "I must get the 'noes' out of the way," and (2) "My trials will help me."

Getting the Noes out of the Way

At Southwestern's sales school I learned that successful selling involves many more negatives than positives. Most people would say no when I asked them to buy my books. A few would say yes. If I could survive the noes, I would eventually find the yeses. To sell books or to survive the ministry, and life, you must know how to get the noes out of the way.

A joke writer for a typical late night television talk show writes about a hundred jokes a day for the host's monologue. That writer said, "If he uses two of my jokes in his opening monologue, I am happy." Therefore, a joke writer with a 98 percent failure rate is a success. Every day he must get ninety-eight noes out of the way to get to two yeses.

Advertising agencies tell us that when a business (or church) mails out a newsletter, 20 percent of its recipients will throw it away; 80 percent will skim the headlines and subheadings; 10 percent to 60 percent will read a short section of copy, copy boxes, and captions; only 1 percent to 10 percent will read the actual text. Thus a successful newsletter is not read by more than 90 percent of its recipients. It takes a great deal of failure to become a success.

Southwestern teachers warned us that most of the doors we knocked on would bring rejection. It was typical to knock on a hundred doors to find ten people at home. Of those ten people who came to the door, maybe two would let us into the house, and one would probably buy. But that one did buy. We made the sale. We were taught to look at all the closed doors, all the noes, as the search for that one who was ready to buy. Whenever we had a closed door, or empty house, or any kind of rejection, we turned away from the door, walked briskly, even joyously out of the yard almost singing, "Wonderful! Just got another no out of the way. I'm closer to finding a yes!"

Don't misunderstand me. I am not equating divine ministry with a man-centered sales talk. Believers do not get up in the morning, gaze proudly into the mirror, and say, "You, my good-looking friend, have great potential. You will do incredible things today!" A Christian that is used of God has a totally opposite outlook. He says, "I am a sinner saved by the grace of God. Without Him I am nothing and I can do nothing. Through Christ, however, I can do whatever He calls me to do" (1 Thess. 5:24).

Getting the noes out of the way is the biblical approach to turning negatives into positives. Christ says that though salvation is offered to many, only a few will truly repent and believe (Matt. 7:13–14). While Christ promises that the fields are white unto harvest (Matt. 9:37), He commands Christians to get the gospel to every creature (Mark 16:15). The Lord is saying, "You must get the noes out of the way to find the yeses." This attitude is crucial to ministry survival. If you look at the no as a personal attack, you may become bitter or even decide to quit. However, if you see the noes as signposts leading the way to the yeses, you can rejoice every time you get one out of the way.

Did you have a new family visit your church for six weeks and then quit coming? You got another no out of the way, which puts you closer to a yes. Did you present a new idea to your church leaders, only to have several voice doubts about its effectiveness? That's okay. You started the decision-making process by getting some noes out of the way. Did you knock on doors for two hours and find no one at home? No problem.

You got some noes out of the way. You are that much closer to the yeses.

The great work of evangelizing the lost is inseparably linked to numbers. We must witness to many folks before we find one who repents. God knows how many souls will respond to His salvation call. Our privilege as ambassadors for Christ is to tell as many as possible that Jesus saves, trusting God for the results. When a soul rejects the truth by refusing a gospel tract or says no to Christ during your sermon invitation, you are getting another no out of the way. God promises that His Word will not return void (Isa. 55:11). Therefore, if you faithfully sow the truth, you have no reason to be discouraged. Though it may sound so, this is not a cold-hearted approach. When sinners reject, of course your heart will break. But even though your emotions will be mixed, it is okay to rejoice when you get a no out of the way. The numbers of souls who say no move you closer to the ones who say yes.

A few years ago I spoke with Leonard, an old friend who was a vital part of a church we planted in the seventies. He reminded me of an afternoon when the two of us were visiting door-to-door. At one house a man was very rude, spoke some harsh words, and slammed the door. According to Leonard, I turned slowly away from that slammed door, almost skipped down the sidewalk saying, "Hallelujah, Leonard! We just got another no out of the way!" He said he has never forgotten that. The silly mental picture of me skipping, thankful to get another no out of the way, helped him survive life's inevitable negatives.

Helpful Trials

God is good to send trials designed to conform you to the image of Christ. There are zero negatives with your good God. He has the power to turn the darkest no into the brightest yes. Trials are not bad because God is not bad. Romans 8:28 promises, "And we know that all things work together for good to them that love God, to them who are the called according to his purpose." The "all things" in that verse includes all the rejection, all the pain, all the disappointments, and all the feelings of failure inevitable in ministry. Do you believe that? If you do, then trials and rejection will not lead to bitterness or despair. Instead, you will often say, "My trials will help me."

God can plant and grow churches anywhere, anytime, using anyone He wants. His main business is not building churches, but people. He can provide continuous success and acceptance in ministry. If He does, praise Him. But normally He ordains trials, often to strengthen you for future challenges. You cannot turn noes into yeses by trusting in yourself, your ability, your cleverness, or your tenacity. You must trust God, Who is building you and your family.

When Paul faced constant trials, I suspect he learned to say, "My trials will help me." Stoned and left for dead, surely he whispered through his pain, "My trials will help me." Three times he received thirty-nine cruel stripes, moaning, "My trials will help me." Shipwrecked, at the mercy of the sea, he must have cried, "My trials will help me!" As the suffering apostle he said, "For I am persuaded, that neither death, nor life, nor angels, nor principalities, nor powers . . . nor any other creature, shall be able to separate us from the love of God, which is in Christ Jesus our Lord" (Rom. 8:38–39). That is a scriptural, positive view of life's negatives. Paul faced much more rejection than acceptance. How did he make it to the finish line, still faithful to God? In part, he survived because he knew his trials would help him. After more than thirty years in the ministry, I can truthfully say that trials, rejection, and negative circumstances have helped me more spiritually than acceptance, praise, and so-called success.

On September 1, 1986, after twelve fruitful years of pastoring a church my wife and I had started in Wisconsin, God directed us into an itinerant ministry of local church evangelism. We sold our house and stuff, purchased an RV and pickup truck, and put our family of five on the road. It was pure adventure—which is what life can be if you are willing to trust God for daily bread. We won't have to live by faith in heaven, so we might as well go for it now.

After we had been on the road for about three months, we received notice that our truck and trailer insurance had been cancelled. The insurance company considered us to be vagabonds with no certain dwelling place or secure income because they didn't understand that we worked for a heavenly Father, Who created and owns the earth (and all insurance companies therein). I immediately began my unforgettable insurance search of 1987. In one month I called a billion or so friends, pastors, businessmen, and insurance companies, with no results. No one was willing to risk insuring the forty-foot-long, 15,000-pound hallway we lived in, even though its driver (me) had only a few vehicle accidents on his record. Imagine that.

I knew God had called us into a revivalist ministry. He had provided a pastor for the church we left behind and miraculously led us to a trailer and truck in a stranger's yard during our two-day search in Indiana. Though I had little experience as an evangelist, we had a full schedule of meetings. Would we have to cancel all our meetings, sell our equipment, and settle down again to pastor a church? The answer came in one remarkable phone call.

While sharing my need with a pastor of a large Chicago church, he interrupted me with these words, "Dave, why don't you join our church? We will make you our staff evangelist, insure your vehicles under our policy, and pray for you." I assured him that I would pray about it. I hung up the phone, prayed about it for about twenty seconds—like Nehemiah's arrow prayer (Neh. 2:4)—and ran to our trailer to tell Claudia of God's incredible provision. We joined that church, and for almost nine years as we traveled in evangelistic work, they provided our truck, trailer, and health insurances. Those folks faithfully prayed for us as we crisscrossed America several times with no major accidents. That negative insurance crisis became one of the most blessed positives of our life.

One of the toughest negatives you face in the pastorate is losing church members. When I was a pastor, I hated that. It was always a trial. No matter why they leave, it hurts a shepherd's heart to say goodbye to sheep. Is it possible to turn this negative into a positive? Absolutely. The usual response to losing folks is "Since God sees the big picture, He must know that their departure will ultimately be for the good of the church. I will simply trust Him and press on with the folks that are still here." This is true. This is right. I have said it myself. But it doesn't always help.

Consider this. Sometimes when people leave, church life improves. The services seem sweeter, the singing brighter, the fellowship deeper. You discover a new freedom in preaching and joy in serving. You might even shed inhibitions you acquired from listening to folks with a critical spirit. Maybe their comments suppressed your personality while you constantly struggled to live up to their expectations. Now they are gone. You are free to be yourself, dependent on God, Who called and equipped you to do His will. If God uses the experience to show you a personal weakness or a needed ministry improvement, respond with an open heart. At the same time, leave room for Him to turn the negative to a positive. Jesus said in Mark 10:18, "No one is good but one, that is, God." Since God is not bad, even the sore trial of losing sheep can become a blessing.

God is only, always good. Get the noes out of the way. Your trials will help you. Let them, and press on.

Living Chapter 6

1. Do you believe your trials will help you? Study the following passages. Ask God to show you that trials can be tools to victory.

    - Genesis 50
    - Romans 5:3–4
    - Romans 8:28–39
    - 2 Corinthians 12:1–10

2. Are you bitter toward God because He has allowed negatives in your life? Get honest, repent, and rejoice that negatives can help you become like Christ: "Dear God, Thank You that You are only good. Thank You that You know what trials I need today to become more like Your Son. Help me to patiently get the noes out of the way so I can get to Your yeses."

3. Are you reaching enough folks to occasionally lose a few? Make a plan to reach more.

4. List areas where you must get past the noes to get to the yeses.

PRESS *ON!* 7

. . . BY VISITING THE PAST

I remembered my mother's prayers. They have clung to me all my life. (Abraham Lincoln)

Remember his marvellous works that he hath done. (Ps. 105:5)

Can you think of someone who talks about his past whenever his mouth is moving? No matter what the topic, the discussion leads to a memory, an anecdote, or a past experience. The moment you start talking about your life, his mind begins to whir. He looks as though he is listening, but he isn't. As soon as you finish a sentence, his mouth begins to move. "That's very interesting. You know, something similar happened to me just a few short decades ago . . ."

Though you may want to run from someone like that (or do something worse), it's true that everyone can benefit from remembering. In chapter 4, I mentioned the remembrance principle—recalling God's goodness in the past can provide encouragement for the present. Let's take a closer look at the power of remembrance. An occasional visit to yesterday can be God's grace tool to help you press on today. After we look at God's biblical servants who knew how to visit the past, we'll see the value of memory and some ways to make energizing visits to the past. God's servants have often encouraged themselves by remembering the past. Whether facing a battle, a new challenge, or even death, they find strength and encouragement in memories.

Bible Leaders Visited the Past

Moses

When God delivered the Israelites from bondage in Egypt, He told Moses to dedicate all the firstborn of man and beast to Him. "Consecrate to me all the firstborn, whatever opens the womb among the children of Israel. . . . It is mine" (Exod. 13:1). Because God had spared the Israelites' firstborn at the Passover, He expected all their firstborn to be dedicated to Him, set apart from all others.

Moses' tough assignment was to motivate the Israelites to make that promise to God. He knew the people were prone to selfishness and fleshly appetites. They might soon forget that He had spared their sons from the death angel and thus be unwilling to dedicate their firstborn to God. To steer them toward obedience and prepare them for the future, Moses said, "Remember this day, in which you came out from Egypt . . . for by strength of hand the LORD brought you out from this place . . ." (Exod. 13:3). "Remember how God delivered your firstborn from death," said Moses. "Let that memory make you grateful to God and give you courage to dedicate your firstborn to Him." Moses enlisted the power of remembrance to move God's people to obey.

Later Moses told the Israelites about God's commandment to remember the Sabbath and keep it holy. Again he called on memories to help them obey. "And remember that thou wast a servant in the land of Egypt, and that the LORD thy

God brought thee out thence through a mighty hand and by a stretched out arm: therefore the LORD thy God commanded thee to keep the sabbath day" (Deut. 5:15). "Remember your slave days," said Moses. "Remember the hard labor and the Egyptian whip. Remember how you longed to be free. Remember Jehovah, Who delivered you. Remember, be thankful, and obey." Moses knew how to take the Israelites on a short, encouraging visit to the past to remember their good God.

David

In Psalm 20, David called on God to be his defense against the enemy. "The LORD hear thee in the day of trouble; the name of the God of Jacob defend thee" (v. 1). Here the psalmist rejoiced in the coming victory and remembered that his strength was in God, not in man or in man-made weapons. "Some trust in chariots, and some in horses: but we will remember the name of the LORD our God" (v. 7). This probably was a chorus to be sung by a choir as a triumphant anthem. It was a reminder that they did not really need chariots or swift horses for victory. All they needed was God. He is also all you need.

In Psalm 105:5 David asked the people to recall God's power and goodness: "Remember his marvellous works that he hath done; his wonders, and the judgments of his mouth." Psalm 78 does the same: "Shewing to the generation to come the praises of the LORD, and his strength, and his wonderful works that he hath done" (v. 4). David was saying, "Remember how God took care of you in past battles. Recall His power and good deeds to your fathers and grandfathers." The singer-writer of the psalms often looked into the memory vault to breathe fresh air encouragement into the present.

Paul

Paul said in Philippians 1:3, "I thank my God upon every remembrance of you." What strikes me about this verse is the all-inclusive word *every*. Did Paul mean he was thankful for everything and everybody in the church of Philippi? Was he thankful for those who opposed him, who gossiped about him, who lied about him? Paul meant what he said. In that amazing statement about the folks of Philippi, he noted that he had only good memories. Every remembrance was one of joy, for which he was grateful.

In his spirit of joy, he implied that nothing bad had happened in Philippi—that everyone supported, followed, and loved him. Actually the Philippian church had some problems. In chapter 1, Paul exhorted them to be others-centered and to work for unity (vv. 9–14), suggesting that they struggled with selfishness and division. In chapter 4 he named two contentious women, Euodias and Syntyche (v. 2). Paul faced negatives in the church of Philippi, but he chose to remember the positives.

Someone has suggested that a person who speaks positively about his childhood is usually an optimist. Though he probably had tough times growing up, he chooses to forget them—to remember only the good. That's how Paul remembered Philippi. His positive visit to the past revealed his God-centered, optimistic spirit.

Like Moses, Paul also used memories to motivate believers to action. He told Timothy he was moved to obey by the memory of Christ's work. "Remember that Jesus Christ of the seed of David was raised from the dead according to my gospel . . . therefore I endure all things for the elect's sake" (2 Tim. 2:8, 10). Paul implied that the rest of us should do the same.

God Tells Us to Visit the Past

God encourages you to enjoy the tool of memory through the ordinances of baptism and the Lord's Supper—sacred activities that are times of memory and dedication. Baptism reminds you that through faith in the atoning blood of Jesus Christ, you share in the death, burial, and resurrection of our Savior. Jesus instituted the Lord's Supper as a memorial of His death. "The

Lord Jesus on the same night in which he was betrayed, took bread . . . and said, Take, eat: this is my body which is broken for you: this do in remembrance of me" (1 Cor. 11:23–24). During baptism and the Lord's Supper, God intends for us to recall their significance, which should move us to carry out their practical implications (dedication of life and gratitude for Christ's sacrifice). When you witness a baptism or take communion, remember His sacrifice, renew yourself, and rejoice in Him. In remembrance, find power to press on.

Visit the Past, but Don't Move In

As I waited for my turn in the dentist's chair recently, I flipped through a large, tattered book entitled *The History of Dentistry*. Looking at the pictures of tooth-extraction methods that resembled medieval torture, I rejoiced that I did not live in the "good old days." Some folks long to move back into the past. Be careful. It is a fine place to visit, but it is a mistake to move in and take up residence. Dwelling continuously on the past may lead to ignoring the realities and responsibilities of the present. Visit the past, but don't move in.

It was Memorial Day, and we were scheduled to be in Kansas City by Wednesday. The trip would take two days, pulling our fifth wheel. We started out early that morning with visions of reaching a St. Louis campground in time for a supper of spare ribs. About thirty miles from St. Louis on I-64, a man in a white pickup pulled up beside us and pointed to our trailer wheels. He looked anxious, excited, and scared.

I glanced into the passenger-side mirror and saw smoke coming from our trailer wheels. Apparently we had blown a tire and the burning rubber was smoking. I slowed down, made it to the next exit, pulled all fifty feet of our rig off onto the shoulder, and shut down the diesel engine. On Memorial Day afternoon, just thirty miles from spare ribs and tranquility, it was not a pretty sight. Things got worse.

The tire was completely destroyed, so I started looking for the spare. I had not searched long when I remembered the words of the friend who had sold me this used trailer in January. "Dave," he had warned, "I carried the spare tire in my truck, so it is not mounted on the trailer like other spare wheels. Don't forget to buy a spare wheel and tire. You don't want to be stuck by the side of the road without a spare."

I had forgotten, and now we were spare-less. No spare tire, no spare ribs, no spare energy. I called 911 on my cell phone and a kind woman shared our predicament with the police department of the closest town—Mascoutah, Illinois. Within minutes an impressive entourage (three squad cars) of law enforcement professionals pulled up next to our wounded RV. A wiry deputy emerged from his vehicle, sauntered over to our exploded tire, and drawled, "Are we having fun yet?" Deputy Barney Fife couldn't have said it better.

The thoughtful officers helped me wire the wheel up off the pavement and then escorted us across the freeway and down Illinois Highway 4 onto Main Street, Mascoutah. With two squad cars in front of us and one bringing up the rear (all with blue lights flashing), we became the second parade the fair citizens of Mascoutah would enjoy on that fine Memorial Day. As we drove slowly down Main Street, folks came out of their houses to admire our home on wheels and wave friendly hellos to my family. It was a gala event. Since it was a day for visiting the past to honor those who had given their lives for our country, I proceeded to remember similar predicaments when we needed God's help with our trailer. He had never failed us. He would not fail us today.

The officers directed us to the parking lot of a large, dark, obviously closed tire store. Lonnie, the owner, was enjoying lunch (probably spare ribs) at the Mascoutah Memorial Day picnic. Someone ran to tell him about our dilemma. Lonnie downed his barbecue, graciously left the picnic, opened his tire store, and sold us a new tire. While he was mounting the tire, the nice woman who ran the gas station next door provided free soft drinks for our needy family. And we did look needy. I was hot, tired and covered with black rubber tire residue. But I was not discouraged. After years of living on the road, I had a memory storehouse of God's loving care of His children. We had dragged our super-sized RV to most states in the USA while raising three children, telling folks about a God Who promises to meet every need.

Remembering the past is not a psychological trick to convince yourself that everything is okay when it is not. It is a biblical tool to conquer fear by girding up the loins of your mind (1 Pet. 1:13). It is consciously making a choice to think instead of just feel. If you are a church planter, you must understand and master this tool of survival that can help you encourage yourself in the Lord. When you stand in the pulpit and see your congregation of twenty-nine people, Satan may whisper in your ear, "Where is your God? You have knocked on hundreds of doors, made thousands of phone calls, and handed out literature for months. There are over fifty thousand people at the football game today and only twenty-nine in your church! Why waste your time when God does not care about you?"

Rather than listen to those discouraging words, recall the marvelous works of God. Remember that one year ago your attendance was not twenty-nine, but nineteen. Remember that though you now meet in a storefront, you used to meet in a school that you had to set up for every service. The nursery was in the hallway and the children's Sunday school class was in the parking lot. Once you had no church sign, no song books, no piano, no offering plates! Recall God's goodness in providing everything, no matter how small, to help your church get going. Recall those who have trusted Christ as Savior in your baby church. Perhaps they have moved out of town or left the church over a misunderstanding, or maybe they are now in a church that condones carnality. That is sad—not a cause for rejoicing. But remember that one day you will rejoice with them in heaven. Satan cannot rob you of your eternal investment in those lives.

Visiting the past is a useful tool for all pastors and full-time ministry servants. If you are a pastor, you know that folks will join your ministry and folks will leave. You can let your memories of people either help you or hurt you. If you listen to Satan, His lies will work via your tough memories to lead you into discouragement or despair. But if you choose to "let this mind be in you which was also in Christ Jesus" (Phil. 2:5), you can think like Christ.

Did Jesus become bitter and angry when Judas betrayed Him and Peter denied Him? No. He pressed on to do God's will and die. Did Paul become bitter and angry when Demas, who "loved this present world" (2 Tim. 4:10), deserted him? No. Paul knew that "all things work together for good to them that love God" (Rom. 8:28). Reject anger toward God because of people who leave or things you lack. Thank Him for who and what you have. Remember the gracious provision of God for you, your family, and your church.

Remind your wife that she is one of the noble ladies whom God has called to lift up the hands of a husband who serves the King. She is the tender heart of the family, so visiting the past will be easy. Encourage her to browse through the scrapbook of her mind, pausing to thank God for every good memory. Challenge her to record in her journal the blessings of God, or to open her computer to those millions of photos of precious children and grandchildren. Recall together the bright days of the past and find joy. We can minister to others by helping them remember the past—answered prayer, God's patience, provision, and promises. Don't move in to the past and take up permanent residence. Make an occasional visit, recall God's goodness, and press on!

Living Chapter 7

1. Make a list of God's past provisions: finances, leading in His will, health, care for your children, protection on the highways, and so forth. Save the list for reading when you feel that God has forgotten you.

2. Do a word search of *remember* or *remembered* in the Bible. Discover people, circumstances, and texts that are encouraging. Some blessed ones are Exodus 2:24; Deuteronomy 5:15; Psalm 25:6; Psalm 63:6; Mark 8:18; Luke 24:6; Ephesians 2:11; and Hebrews 10:17.

3. Start a book of remembrance and record answers to prayer and God's provision for your needs.

PRESS *ON!*

.... WITH HELP FROM THE LAWS OF THE HARVEST

8

Don't judge each day by the harvest you reap, but by the seeds that you plant. (Robert Louis Stevenson)

Let us not be weary in well doing: for in due season we shall reap, if we faint not. (Gal. 6:9)

I loved to ride the roller coaster at our Memphis amusement park. The Pippin, a wooden clacker and whizzer, was more fun than my tenth birthday party. Slow breathing and bulging eyes got me to the top of the first hill; screaming with eyes closed took me to the bottom. Up and down it went, like a ship on rough seas. My total investment for three minutes of fun: five cents!

Full-time ministry servants ride roller coasters, too—emotional ones—and they aren't as much fun as The Pippin. You are at a peak, reveling in joy, contentment, and victory when the phone rings. After the disgruntled church member finishes talking at you, you hang up the phone and are in a valley of discouragement. The ministry has you rejoicing one moment and hurting the next.

God's laws of the harvest—sowing and reaping—provide stability on the ministry roller coaster. They are sobering, strengthening, and continuously at work in everyone. Each of us, without exception, is sowing and reaping every day, every hour.

There are at least seven laws of the harvest, summarized in these Bible texts.

> Be not deceived; God is not mocked: for whatsoever a man soweth, that shall he also reap. For he that soweth to his flesh shall of the flesh reap corruption; but he that soweth to the Spirit shall of the Spirit reap life everlasting. And let us not be weary in well doing: for in due season we shall reap, if we faint not. (Gal. 6:7–9)

> But this I say, he which soweth sparingly shall reap also sparingly; and he which soweth bountifully shall reap also bountifully. (2 Cor. 9:6)

Like a farmer who enjoys fruit via God's agricultural harvest laws, you can reap multitudes of spiritual blessings through His laws of sowing and reaping.

Law #1—You Reap Only What You Sow

> Be not deceived; God is not mocked: for whatsoever a man soweth, that shall he also reap. (Gal. 6:7)

A farmer must plant seed to harvest a crop. He would be presumptuous to "pray in faith" over his land and refuse to plant seed. Though he may be a man of unusual faith, God still expects him to sow seed, spread fertilizer, and weed the field—while praying fervently for the results. If you want to reap a harvest, you must sow seed.

God told Abraham in Genesis 12:1 that if he would leave his country and kindred, He would make him the father of a great nation. Abraham sowed in faith by gathering his family and leaving the land he loved; eventually he reaped the promised nation. God told Moses to get up in the morning, go down to the edge of the river, confront Pharaoh, and say, "Let my people go, that they may serve me in the wilderness" (Exod. 7:16). Moses sowed obedience, and God liberated the children of Israel. Jesus did more than just announce that He had come to do the will of His Father. He sowed the seed of salvation by suffering, bleeding, and dying. He was obedient to the death of the cross. The result—one day every knee shall bow to Him (Phil. 2:8–10). All reaping requires sowing.

Does this mean that you reap only what you have personally sown? No. You often benefit from seed sown by others. Attend a Memorial Day service or walk through a military cemetery, and thank God that you did not have to fight in the Revolutionary War or trudge ashore at Normandy. Enjoy the Fourth of July fireworks with gratitude that you can preach in a public gathering, cast a secret ballot, even own a gun—freedoms painfully purchased by your forefathers.

We all benefit from our parents' sowing in our lives. When I was eight years old, my dad took thirty-five cents from his pocket, my first weekly allowance. He then offered careful instruction about tithing, which became my habit. Each time I mowed our neighbor's yard, I gave 10 percent to our church. By the time I landed my coveted ice cream parlor job at age twelve, tithing was easy. I still practice it as the basis of my personal biblical stewardship. It is a habit I find easy because of seed sown by my dad.

Christ sowed seeds of your eternal life by dying on the cross. He did not ask you to join Him there, but you can enjoy the blessings of salvation. Repentance and faith provide eternal benefits. Thank God for all who sowed seed that you might reap blessings today.

Though you enjoy dividends of seed sown by others, most of God's blessings come to those who sow. James said, "Ye have not, because ye ask not" (James 4:2). Likewise, Jesus instructed, "Ask, and it shall be given you; seek, and ye shall find" (Matt. 7:7). If you want to reap, you must be willing to sow. Two bonuses from this principle are that you can choose what you want to reap and that no matter how tough life is, you can always sow.

Before planting, a farmer plans for the harvest so that he can purchase and plant the right seeds. You do the same for your backyard garden—plan, make a list, purchase seeds, and plant. God gives you the same privilege in your life and ministry!

Make a list of your spiritual goals. Then open your Bible to find the seed God expects you to sow. Do you want to reap children who seek after God? Sow seeds of biblical love, godly example, loving discipline, and faithful instruction in righteousness (study Proverbs). Do you want to reap a life of faith-adventure? Sow seeds of consistent, fervent prayer (James 5:16). Do you long to have financial freedom? Sow seeds of biblical giving (1 Cor. 4:2). Are you hungry to reap souls that you personally win? Sow seeds of evangelism by being soul-conscious, giving out tracts, and talking to folks about their souls (Acts 1:8). Decide what you want to reap and sow the appropriate seed.

No matter how you feel, you can always sow. Right now, ministry trials may have you thinking, "I just don't feel like doing anything." No matter how dark the day, how tough the trial, or how heavy your spirit, you can always do something. Sometimes circumstances seem so overwhelming that you can do nothing but collapse on the floor and pray. So do it! Even then, you will be sowing seed.

Claudia and I planted our first church while in our early twenties. We didn't just *feel* inexperienced and stupid. We were! Occasionally I would awake at night and worry. How could I pastor this baby, yet growing, church with my limited experience? How could I manage our first building project? I had been pretty good with Tinker Toys and Lincoln Logs, but this would have to be a real building with rooms, carpet, paint, pews—and a mortgage. It was scary. On top of all that, I had my flesh to contend with every day. What was I to do?

Though I couldn't work on practical problems in the middle of the night, there was something I *could* do. I could get out of my bed and pray. In the main room of our two-room apartment sat our wood-framed, orange-cushioned sofa. It was the focal point of our living room/kitchen/dining room/office. Though our apartment was very cozy (so small that the phone cord would stretch from the back wall to the front), we loved it. That orange sofa became my place to pray—my place to do something during nights of anxious care. At that couch, I sowed seed, relying on the laws of the harvest.

You may be hurting, discouraged, confused, or angry. You may feel helpless, powerless, even worthless. You may have no idea how to solve your problem. But you can do something. You can pray! Enter the presence of your King and sow seeds of peace, wisdom, power, and victory. He promises that if you sow, you will reap. Make a Holy Spirit–directed list of ministry goals. Pray over them. That is foundational sowing—much like a farmer plowing the soil.

Of course, after you sow seeds of prayer, do more than pray. Elijah prayed and then preached truth to King Ahab. Daniel prayed and then announced judgment to Nebuchadnezzar. Nehemiah's wall-building team prayed, then labored day and night on the wall. Paul prayed without ceasing and then spent his life traveling, preaching, and planting churches. Get out into the field and sow the appropriate seed. Water it with constant prayer and expect a harvest.

Law #2—You Reap in the Same Kind as You Sow

Galatians 6:8 says, "For he that soweth to his flesh shall of the flesh reap corruption; but he that soweth to the Spirit shall of the Spirit reap life everlasting." The farmer knows that if he plants squash, he will reap squash. (If he is a member of your church, you probably will too.) Corn plants produce corn. Bean seeds grow into beans, not watermelons. This second law says you will reap in the same kind as you sow. If you sow to the flesh, you will reap fleshly results. If you sow to the Spirit, you will enjoy spiritual blessings.

This principle is first mentioned in Genesis 1:12, which says, "And the earth brought forth grass, and herb yielding seed after his kind, and the tree yielding fruit, whose seed was in itself, after his kind: and God saw that it was good." Verse 21 says, "And God created great whales, and every living creature that moveth, which the waters brought forth abundantly, after their kind, and every winged fowl after his kind: and God saw that it was good." Animals and plants reproduce in the same kind.

Nicodemus, a proud, unregenerate Pharisee, approached Jesus one night looking for spiritual satisfaction. Jesus knew his heart condition and immediately confronted him with his need to be born again. He said in John 3:3, "Verily, verily, I say unto thee, Except a man be born again, he cannot see the kingdom of God." Nicodemus didn't get it. He thought Jesus was talking about physical birth. Jesus' further explanation, based on this second law of the harvest, was "That which is born of the flesh is flesh; and that which is born of the Spirit is spirit" (John 3:6). Nicodemus was a Pharisee, trusting his good works to save his soul. Jesus revealed that his works were useless. "Nicodemus," noted Jesus, "you will reap the same kind as you sow. Works of the flesh will produce nothing but fleshly results. You must be born from on high (regenerated) to see the kingdom of heaven."

This law is operative not only in salvation but also in daily Christian living. It is sobering to acknowledge that you often reap the same kind as you sow. Negatively, if you sow seeds of anger, bitterness, selfishness, lying, lust, jealousy, and so forth, you may reap those same maladies in some form of daily life.

I am thankful there is a blessed flip side of this law. Sow spiritual seed; reap spiritual blessings. Be kind to someone; someone will be kind to you. Offer mercy to an offender; someday someone will show mercy to you. Pray faithfully for a friend; others will pray for you. Give and it will be given back to you.

If you want to reap souls for Christ, should you sow conversations about weather, sports, and politics? Those topics are fine if they lead to planting the gospel seed, but alone, they will not produce souls because you reap in the same kind as you sow. Tomato plants produce tomatoes, squash begets squash (lots of it), and you must sow to the gospel to reap souls (Matt. 9:37–38). To have victory over the flesh, sow seeds of personal holiness (Gal. 5:16). If you sow Spirit-filled communication in your marriage, you will reap mutual edification (Eph. 4:29). Sowing to the Spirit will bring a harvest of spiritual results. Decide what you want to reap. Discover what specific seeds you need to sow. Start sowing. You will reap in the same kind as you sow.

Law #3—You Reap More than You Sow

"For he that soweth to his flesh shall of the flesh reap corruption; but he that soweth to the Spirit shall of the Spirit reap life everlasting" (Gal. 6:8). This law promises that you will reap more than you sow. The farmer relies on this. Not all his seed will grow. Some falls on bad soil and some is eaten by birds. But some does take root, producing more than he sowed.

How much flesh does one have to sow to reap corruption, or eternal death? What must a man do to go to hell? The answer is—not much. He does not have to become a blasphemer, an atheist, or a bitter, hateful person. Nor must he lead a lifetime crusade to discredit Christianity. All he must do is reject the Holy Spirit's wooing to repent and receive the Savior (John 3:18), and at death he will reap much more than he sowed (Rev. 20:15). What must one do to be sure of eternal life? Simply trust Christ as Savior (John 3:16). A supernatural, Spirit-led prayer of repentance and faith guarantees heaven. The believer reaps infinitely more than he sowed in that one moment of calling on the name of Jesus Christ (Rom. 10:13).

Two key passages offer strong warnings about reaping more than you sow. Proverbs 22:8 says, "He that soweth iniquity shall reap vanity [falsehood, fraud, sorrow, wickedness]: and the rod of his anger shall fail." Those who sow iniquity (any kind of evil) will reap a harvest of adversity (grief, suffering, and anxiety). In Hosea 8:7, the prophet warns Israel, "For they have sown the wind, and they shall reap the whirlwind." The Hebrew intensive form indicates that though they sowed a gentle wind, they will reap a powerful hurricane. Hosea says that often the consequences are greater than the deed, like the whirlwind is greater than the wind.

Let the warnings of Solomon and Hosea deter you from sin. Consider the consequences of yielding to the flesh. Meditate on those who will be disappointed, disillusioned, or even depressed by your transgression. Some may use your failure as an excuse to sin. Others may begin to doubt the goodness or even the existence of God. You will reap more than you sow—more than you can imagine.

The life of David painfully illustrates this law. He sowed one bad seed in his mind by gazing at Bathsheba taking a bath on her rooftop (2 Sam. 11:2). Soon he broke five of the ten commandments: he coveted another man's wife, stole her for himself, committed adultery, lied about his sin, and committed murder by ordering Bathsheba's husband to fight on the front line of battle.

In 2 Samuel, Nathan the prophet informed David that he was the guilty one who had failed God (12:7). He then pronounced a threefold judgment on the king, noting that David had essentially killed Uriah (one man), yet the sword would not depart from David's entire household (12:11). Next, he reminded David that he had taken Uriah's wife (one woman), but soon all his wives would be taken. As if that were not enough, Nathan announced that David had committed his sin in "secret," but his wives were to be defiled in public (12:12). Nathan also prophesied that the king would be required to repay his sin debt fourfold. That happened, and David lost four sons in death: Shimea (12:19), Amnon (13:28–29), Absalom (18:14), and Adonijah (1 Kings 2:24–25). David reaped more than he sowed in one night of sin.

In junior high school I played my guitar and sang folk music with my best friend, Ron. Ron's uncle was the public relations director for Hart's Bread, a local company. He hired us to record a Christmas advertising jingle, paying us a whopping $25 each to strum and sing the following award-losing jingle:

> Daddy buys the bacon, Mama makes the bed,
> Santa fills the stocking, and Hart's makes the bread.
> Hart's makes the biscuits, and Hart's makes the buns,
> Hart's makes eating a mighty lot of fun.
> Hart's makes the biscuits, and Hart's makes the buns,
> Hart's makes eating [big ending here] a . . . mighty . . . lot . . . of . . . fun!

Ron wrote the music using our favorite (and only) three guitar chords: C, F, and G7. The taping in the studio was going so well that Ron, in what he proclaimed to be a Carnegie Hall moment, decided to sing harmony on our big ending. Knowing as much about music theory as he did about brain surgery, Ron chose a random harmony-sounding note from the G7 chord on his guitar. It was not until later when the ad aired on the radio that we realized he had chosen the wrong note.

Each time the jingle played, it would begin with the announcer saying, "And now, for Hart's Bread, here's Ron and Dave!" Then followed enthusiastic canned applause and cheers as we played a typical Memphis-style guitar-pickin' introduction. After the jingle aired about a million times, one of my friends at school pulled me aside and told me in hushed tones that while listening to his radio he heard the all-too familiar announcement, "And now, for Hart's Bread, here's Ron and Dave!" The disc jockey, live at the microphone, chimed in and said, "Oh no, not again!" As the applause and cheering crowd began, he added, "Keep clapping and maybe they'll go away." So much for our recording career. We reaped much more than we sowed with that one wrong note.

Rejoice in the positive application of this law—you will also reap more than you sow to the good. Though you may often feel inadequate in ministry, if you are faithful to sow spiritual seed, God will multiply your efforts. Though you feel weak of faith, keep on praying. You will see more answers than you expected. Do you feel ill-equipped for the challenges of the ministry? Keep on doing His will. You will reap more than you sow. Keep on teaching kids who seem uninterested. Keep on preaching to folks who look like they'd rather be fishing. Are you discouraged because of sin in your life? Repent, enjoy God's grace and forgiveness, and get back to work. Abraham, Paul, Peter, and even Christ, had to deal with the weakness of the flesh, yet they accomplished the work God called them to do. Eternity will reveal their harvest, and yours.

Planting a church in Tennessee in the nineties was tough. God got the church up and running within six years, but those years were difficult. Claudia and I occasionally got so discouraged that we questioned our call. Were we accomplishing anything? Did God really call us to plant in a city with over eight hundred other Baptist churches? How could we compete with mega-churches that offered Jesus in a package with worldly entertainments and little commitment? We kept sowing spiritual seed though, and God blessed. By the tenth anniversary of our first service God had multiplied the sown seed. Of those early church members, one became a full-time evangelist. One couple were missionaries to Native Americans, and another worked to reach American Muslims. A man who had received Christ in the first month of the church was faithfully, with the help of his son, conducting a bus ministry to children. Many others were going on for God.

During most of those six years we felt as though we were struggling up a rocky precipice, but God multiplied our efforts. He promises that you will reap more than you sow.

Law #4—You Reap in a Different Season than You Sow

"And let us not be weary in well doing, for in due season we shall reap if we faint not" (Gal. 6:9). God promises that the harvest will come, but only in His time. The farmer understands this. He may work for weeks plowing the land, preparing the soil, and planting the seed. Does He expect an immediate harvest? He knows God's laws of nature take time. He must wait for rain, sunshine, heat, and cold to bring the seed to harvest. But the harvest will eventually come: "While the earth remaineth, seedtime and harvest, and cold and heat, and summer and winter, and day and night shall not cease" (Gen. 8:22). I agree with whoever said that God's promises are certain, but they do not all mature in ninety days.

Solomon said, "Cast thy bread upon the waters; for thou shalt find it after many days" (Eccles. 11:1). Casting bread on water refers to sowing on damp or wet ground. This is "an allusion to the sowing of rice, which was sown upon muddy ground, or ground covered with water, and trodden in by the feet of cattle; it thus took root, and grew, and was found after many days in a plentiful harvest."[1] Our daughter spent a few days in rural

---

1. Adam Clark Commentary PowerBible 5.6.

China helping with the annual rice planting. She was taught to wade into the water, lean down, and press the seedlings into a flooded paddy. Though her rows were not as straight as those who were experienced, her friends promised the harvest would come in a later season. She cast her bread upon the waters, where the farmers expected to find it after many days. God will reward you for your labor, but He will send the harvest when He chooses.

This law of different-season reaping is both a negative warning and an encouraging blessing. Negatively, it is foolish to delay repentance. Ecclesiastes 8:11 says, “Because sentence against an evil work is not executed speedily, therefore the heart of the sons of men is fully set in them to do evil.” Because of your flesh, you may minimize sin and think you have gotten away with evil. But God promises are true. Later, you will reap. *God promises!*

God told the Israelites to let the land rest every seventh year, but they disobeyed. He pronounced judgment: “And I will scatter you among the heathen, and will draw out a sword after you: and your land shall be desolate, and your cities waste. Then shall the land enjoy her sabbaths, as long as it lieth desolate, and ye be in your enemies’ land; even then shall the land rest, and enjoy her sabbaths” (Lev. 26:33–34). God did not immediately punish them, waiting almost five hundred years before removing Israel from the land through the Babylonian captivity (and letting the land rest for seventy years). God waited five centuries to collect His dues.

The wisest response to sin is prompt repentance (1 John 1:9). Those five hundred years were just a moment to God. So is one man’s lifetime. Some men spend their lives in selfish pursuits, promising God that when they retire they will give time to Him. Retirement comes, but death follows quickly, leaving no time to serve God, or even enjoy retirement. Could it be that God has patiently waited to exact judgment? Only He knows.

Positively, you can afford to be patient and wait for the harvest! Don't be discouraged if you do not have immediate ministry results. Do all the good you can for as long as you can and wait on God for results. Keep on sowing ministry seed through praying, witnessing, tract distribution, teaching, preaching, studying, writing, and counseling.

When I was a young pastor, I flew to Scotland for a preaching conference. The plane was spacious, the seats comfortable, and the service excellent. I had my own headset with a variety of musical genres, gourmet food with unlimited coffee, access to pillows and blankets, and even an in-flight movie. It was luxury. I enjoyed the preaching conference, but in retrospect, the journey was more fun than the destination! God may delay your harvest because the wait will help you more than the actual harvest. As you wait, spend extra time praying, which will bring you closer to Him. Let God use the time to build, strengthen, and nourish your faith. Getting closer to God is worth much more than any harvest. Enjoy the trip and grow as you wait.

Several years after leaving our Wisconsin church plant, a member told us of a woman who received Christ one Sunday morning. The new convert said, "Nine years ago, Claudia Barba knocked on my door and told me about this church. It took me a while, but I finally decided to visit." After nine years, the seed produced a harvest. Like most evangelists, I love to see evidence that God is working. I prefer seeing immediate results. Sometimes that happens, but normally, the harvest comes later. I am learning to wait, remembering that God's timing is always perfect. Be content to sow the seed and wait. You will reap in a different season than you sow.

Law #5—You Reap in Proportion to Your Sowing

In 2 Corinthians 8–9, Paul challenged the Corinthians to contribute to the offering he was collecting for poor believers in Jerusalem. In 9:6 he mentioned a harvest law to motivate them to generous giving. "He which soweth sparingly shall reap also sparingly; and he which soweth bountifully shall reap also bountifully." The primary reference is to finances, but the application is broad. Paul says if you sow a little, you will reap a little. If you sow a lot, you will reap a lot. That is, you reap in proportion to your sowing. The farmer knows from experience, the more seed he sows, the more crop he will harvest.

Though the maxim "you get what you pay for" is not found in the Bible, it is biblical. Spiritual blessings require spiritual investment. According to Psalm 84:11, obedience is a key to God's blessing. "For the LORD God is a sun and shield: the LORD will give grace and glory: no good thing will he withhold from them that walk uprightly." God promises to not withhold the good things he has planned for you—if you walk uprightly (obey). Apparently, His blessings are bestowed in proportion to obedience. If you pray occasionally, you may see a few answers to prayer, but if you pray without ceasing, answers will be continuous. If you share the gospel once or twice a year, you may lead a few souls to Christ. But if you are always soul-conscious, always sowing gospel seeds, you will win more for Him. This is proportionate sowing and reaping.

The previous harvest law, "reap in a different season than you sow," is dependent on God's faithfulness. He will give the harvest in His time. This law is dependent on your faithfulness. Both laws are simultaneously true and active. God will multiply whatever seed is sown, but you must sow all the good you can. "The liberal soul shall be made fat: and he that watereth shall be watered also himself" (Prov. 11:25). Sow liberally and expect a generous harvest.

> If you want to be rich—give!
> If you want to be poor—grasp!
> If you want abundance—scatter!
> If you want to be needy—hoard!

You will reap in proportion to your sowing in prayer, in outreach, in time spent with your wife and children, in sermon preparation, in efforts to mature spiritually, in everything. An essential area for you to sow liberally is in time spent alone with God. It is here that you gird up the loins of your mind and gain strength to handle Satan's efforts to hinder you (Ps. 1:1–3; 119:9, 11; Josh. 1:8). Don't neglect your morning devotions. Through careful Bible study and focused prayer you sow seeds of truth—to reap a harvest of victory throughout the day.

From childhood I dreamed of piloting an airplane. My dream came true while pastoring in Wisconsin. To earn my private pilot's license, I spent Mondays logging hours toward my first solo flight. After more lessons and flying time, I was ready for the final exercise required for my license—a solo cross-country flight. It would be a three-legged adventure from Milwaukee to Wassau, Wisconsin, down to Dubuque, Iowa, and then back to Milwaukee.

On a crisp, autumn afternoon I rented a Cessna 150, filed my flight plan and took off. The first leg of the flight went well, and I landed in Wassau. I filed another plan and took off for Dubuque. As I lifted off the runway, I mentally patted myself on the back for my successful beginning. Pride can be dangerous, though—especially for a pilot. (Prov. 16:18 warns, "Pride goeth before destruction, and an haughty spirit before a fall.")

About thirty miles northeast of Dubuque, I radioed the airport and listened carefully to the air traffic controller as he told me the wind direction, the barometric pressure, and the active runway. I mentally logged the wind and pressure information, then jotted down the runway number for landing. As you may know, the big numbers painted on the threshold of airport runways correspond to the degrees on a compass. Runway 18 is 180 degrees, which is due south. Runway 36 is 360 degrees, or due north, and so on.

About five miles from the airport, I called the air traffic controller. "Dubuque tower, this is Cessna three two uniform (32U) for landing."

"Cessna three two uniform," replied the tower, "continue on."

The directive to "continue on" was new to me. I should have asked him to explain it. That would have been smart. However, I figured he was a busy man in a busy airport. I didn't want to bother him. That was not smart. Soon I had the airport in sight. I knew the active runway, so I landed the plane. On the ground, as I slowed to a stop I noticed some trucks and workers about seventy-five feet in front of me in the runway. That was not normal. Suddenly my radio crackled to life with the voice of the air traffic controller, "Three two uniform, where are you?"

This is not a good question for an air traffic controller to ask a pilot he is tracking in his airspace. I replied, "I am on the ground."

"Sir, you need to taxi to the nearest hanger and give me a call," he said.

I taxied in, shut down my engine, and called the man. We had a memorable conversation. "Sir, do you know what you just did?"

"No," I muttered.

"You just landed on the taxiway."

The taxiway is not the runway. The runway is the big, wide, typically concrete road with big numbers painted on each end. The taxiway is the little road, often dirt or gravel, that you drive the airplane on to get to and from the runways. You are supposed to land the plane on the runway, not the taxiway. Then the friendly air traffic controller said something I will never forget: "You know, sir, no one has ever done that before."

Not only had I landed the plane before being cleared to land but I also committed a technical error. The Cessna 150 was equipped with two compasses: a magnetic one (like a Boy Scout compass) and a gyroscopic one (a mechanical instrument). When flying close to the earth in a small plane, the gyroscopic compass, affected by gravity, can become inaccurate. It must be occasionally recalibrated during flight. I had failed to do that. When I got within landing distance of the airport, I glanced at my gyro, which was not accurate, and landed on what I thought was the active runway. My could-have-been-fatal mistake was this: I failed to true the variable gyro compass to the absolute magnetic one. It could have cost my license—or my life. By God's grace, all I did was land on the wrong "runway."

Here's the importance, the necessity, of spending time each morning in God's Word. Your heart is subject to the powerful pull of evil. If you get up in the morning and take off into ministry without recalibrating your heart to the absolutes of the Word, you may end up landing on the wrong runway. Sad to say, some have neglected personal soul-nurturing in the Word and crashed, losing their testimony, negating their ministry. Take time to true your ever-changing heart to God's admonitions, instructions, and promises. You will reap in proportion to your sowing.

Law #6—You Reap the Good If You Persevere; the Evil Comes to Harvest on Its Own

Does the farmer notice his neighbor's weeds and enviously say, "I need to buy some weed seeds so I can have lovely weeds like his?" Must the farmer work hard to have weeds among his crops? Weeds require no work or planting. They appear all by themselves, sometimes overnight. However, the farmer does have to labor to bring the seed to harvest. He must persevere through drought, hungry animals, pesky insects, plant diseases, damaging winds, and crop-destroying hail.

You don't have to do anything to be plagued by weeds of sin. Evil, since it is found in the heart, is present by default (Jer. 17:9). Adam started it, and you must deal with it until death. The parable of the tares (Matt. 13:24–30) makes it clear that "while men slept, his enemy came and sowed tares among the wheat, and went his way" (13:25). Satan is working full-time to sow tares in your heart. You don't have to do it yourself.

Though you don't have to work at doing wrong, if you want to enjoy a blessed harvest, you must not faint. "And let us not be weary in well doing: for in due season we shall reap, if we faint not" (Gal. 6:9). This should affect your attitude toward exhausting ministry trials. Since God, Who is only good, never sends a bad thing into your life, you can accurately view every trial as His custom-made tool to conform you to His image. Persevere. View the trial as a friend rather than an enemy.

Church planter, you must live by this law. You struggle through the early years of the new church, spending all your time and energy sowing seed. When trials come and challenges multiply, if you quit you will miss the harvest. This is also true for the pastor of an established church. You faithfully preach, teach, and sow seeds of spiritual growth for years. Then Satan sows tares of discord. If you give up in discouragement, you may forfeit a fruitful harvest that is just around the corner. If your present conflict is God prompting you to move to another field of service, He will make it clear. Until then, patiently persevere.

When our family traveled the country in itinerant evangelism, we loved to hike the trails of state and national parks. Sometimes, to get to the other shore of a fast-moving stream, we would have to step from one slippery, moss-covered rock to another. We would tell our children to hold our hands and watch each step. We promised that if they would trust us, hold tight, and follow our lead, they would soon reach the other shore. Your trials may just be stepping stones through swift waters that will lead you to a harvest on the other shore. Don't rush God and miss the harvest. Just as you want God to be patient with you, be patient and wait on Him. In due season, you will reap if you faint not.

Law #7—You Cannot Change Today's Harvest, but You Can Begin Working on Tomorrow's

If you focus exclusively on the past, the laws of the harvest can be discouraging. Satan may send thoughts like these:

- "Since I sowed bad seed in my life, I am reaping a harvest of pain and judgment. I have no hope."
- "It is all my fault that my kids do not love God. I did not sow enough good seed in their lives when they were young."
- "My marriage is shaky because of bad habits and attitudes that I have sown. I may as well throw in the towel."

Though there may be some truth in those statements, God does not want you to live in bondage to your past. Though Paul had sowed some bad seed in his lifetime, he refused to let his past control him. In Philippians 3:13, he said, "Brethren, I count not myself to have apprehended: but this one thing I do, forgetting those things which are behind, and reaching forth unto those things which are before."

Your life today is a result of what you sowed yesterday, last week, and last month. Your pain, heartbreak, discouragement, or chastening is probably the product of bad seed sown in the past. It is true that some sins produce long-lasting consequences. However, since God lives today and loves you forever, it is time to get over the past. Do not let your past control your present. Fretting about it will produce nothing but crippling feelings of failure. If you have unconfessed sin, ask forgiveness and get on with life (1 John 1:9). If you have wrongs that need to be righted, take care of them. Take advantage of God's grace, plant good seed today, and anticipate a glorious harvest. Reconcile with someone you have offended. Open communication with your spouse. Teach godliness and character to your children. Share the gospel. Get counsel and make a plan for victory over your besetting sin. Pray. Spend time in the Word. You cannot change today's harvest, but you can work on the one that will come.

God's laws of the harvest are absolute, powerful, and life changing. Study them; understand them; let them be deterrents to sin and channels to blessing. You may need to ask forgiveness for bad seed that you are sowing and begin preparing for a future spiritual harvest by sowing good seed in specific areas. Begin now to live each hour in light of the laws of the harvest.

Living Chapter 8

1. Search the Bible, especially the Old Testament, for examples of sowing and reaping.

2. List the seven laws of the harvest on a 3 x 5 card to memorize.

3. Meditate thoughtfully to discover examples of sowing and reaping in your personal life.

4. List ways you are now sowing bad seed.

5. List specific good seed you need to begin sowing today. Promise God to start preparing for tomorrow's harvest.

6. Pray, "Father, forgive me for sowing bad seed. I realize that I will reap in the same kind as I sow. Give me grace to begin sowing godly seed that will produce a harvest of spiritual blessings."

PRESS *ON!*

. . . ONE DAY AT A TIME

Live one day at a time and make it a masterpiece. (Dale West)

Blessed be the LORD, who daily loadeth us with benefits, even the God of our salvation. (Ps. 68:19)

During a Wednesday night church service, the pastor asked for prayer requests. Folks requested prayer for employment, wisdom for decisions, and salvation for unsaved relatives. Then a new church member stood. His wife sat in the pew with her head down. "Please pray for us," he began. "Today's medical tests showed that our eight-year-old daughter has some form of leukemia. Or maybe bone cancer. Pray that God will give the doctor . . . wisdom . . . and . . . give us . . . strength."

Pastor, if that was your church, you probably would have replied, "Thanks for sharing your burden with us. We will all pray. We are grateful to know that God is in control."

But what would you have been thinking, along with other members who heard the request? "How will they survive this incredible trial? They will endure endless tests, sleepless nights, and extended hospital stays—not to mention financial stress. And at the end of it, maybe a funeral. How will they make it? How will they survive? Will they be able to press on?"

The comforting answer for that family is this: God will give grace for their trial. It will be divinely designed, perfectly suited to their spiritual temperament and temperature. And it will be daily grace, for God expects us to live just one day at a time. If that couple knew all the details of the trial at once, they would be overwhelmed. But God promises grace to press on one day at a time.

Today Is All God Requires

The "one day at time" principle is an encouraging, biblical key to survival. When God created the earth, He gave the gift of day and night. "And God called the light Day, and the darkness he called Night. And the evening and the morning were the first day" (Gen. 1:5). After working one day at a time for six, He rested for a day.

In Exodus 16, "The whole congregation of the children of Israel murmured against Moses and Aaron in the wilderness. . . . Would to God we had died by the hand of the LORD in the land of Egypt" (vv. 2–3). God miraculously sent food, but in His wisdom He did not supply provisions for a year, or month, or a week. "Behold, I will rain bread from heaven for you; and the people shall go out and gather a certain rate every day, that I may prove them, whether they will walk in my law, or no" (Exod. 16:4). He sent manna each morning. They were to gather just enough for that day.

God sent a pillar of cloud, one day at a time, to guide the Israelites (Exod. 40:38). Solomon warns about trying to deal with more than one day at a time: "Boast not thyself of to morrow; for thou knowest not what a day may bring forth" (Prov. 27:1). Jesus counsels us to focus on today, not to worry about tomorrow: "Take therefore no thought for the morrow: for the morrow shall take thought for the things of itself. Sufficient unto the day is the evil thereof" (Matt. 6:34).

God must have considered man's weakness when he established seasons and separated day from night. Imagine the burden of living life as one unbroken day! In the night you enjoy respite from burdens, rebuild damaged body cells, and rejuvenate your store of energy. Jeremiah reminds us that God's mercies are new every morning (Lam. 3:23). The dawn of a new day usually provides inspiration to press on.

God made animals to benefit from His one-day-at-time blessing. The migratory pattern of the arctic tern takes him around the globe. This fifteen-inch bundle of energy starts near the North Pole and flies twenty-two-thousand miles in a year. He has a voracious appetite, so he follows food-bearing ocean currents. When fishermen spot the tern, they know that fish are near. How does the tern fly around the earth? He breaks down his long, annual journey into small, daily assignments, flying a set number of miles each day. On and on he goes, day after day, until he reaches his goal. God created the tern, and you, to survive by taking one challenge at a time, one trial at a time, one day at a time.

Ephesians 5:18 commands, "And be not drunk with wine . . . but be filled with the Spirit." To survive one day at a time, work at living a Spirit-filled life. The filling of the Spirit is not a one-time action but a continuous work of grace. This present active imperative form of the verb *be filled* (do it now!) challenges you to live a continuous Spirit-filled life. God does not promise that today's anointing is effective for life. You must continuously confess sin (1 John 1:9), asking for immediate, moment-by-moment fullness. Strength to press on is available one day, one moment, at a time.

Daily Trials

I have discussed the value of trials. Understanding their value, memorizing verses of encouragement, even hanging inspirational sayings on your bathroom mirror, will not prevent trials. They are a normal, necessary part of progressive sanctification. You need them to become like the Savior, Who faced trials until His final breath. You can survive and benefit from your trials as you deal with them one day at a time. Paul said, "For which cause we faint not; but though our outward man perish, yet the inward man is renewed day by day. For our light affliction, which is but for a moment, worketh for us a far more exceeding and eternal weight of glory" (2 Cor. 4:16–17).

Though your inward man, or spirit, may be discouraged by trials, God promises to renew your spirit one day at a time. God sent Moses to the desert for forty years to prepare him to lead the Israelites out of Egypt. How did he survive long, lonely days-nights-weeks-months-years in the desert? One day at a time! God visited Moses when he was lonely. Choirs of angels sang him to sleep. Moses occasionally reasoned that if he could survive one more day, God would lead him out of the desert. Moses did make it one more day. And another. And another. One day at a time added up to a week, then a month, and a year. One morning Moses awoke to find that forty years had passed. At the burning bush, God put Moses back on the front line (Exod. 3:2ff.).

God will send what you need to comfort and heal your hurting spirit. It may be a phone call from a friend, a book from your shelf, a radio sermon, or a God-given song in the night. God's everlasting love (Jer. 31:3) will never leave you comfortless. All He asks is that you trust Him throughout this one day.

Daily Temptations

Jesus understands your fierce temptations because He already endured each one. He sympathetically instructs you to pray daily, "Lead us not into temptation, but deliver us from evil." Just as you ask for daily bread, ask also for victory over evil. Since Satan is mean and tireless and hates God, your early morning prayer does not guarantee victory. Throughout the day you must call upon God. He always listens and promises a way to escape, one temptation at a time (1 Cor. 10:13).

Do you struggle with a besetting sin (Heb. 12:1)? Have you justified it for years? You know it is wrong. Your inward man detests it. Your heart is broken when you yield. You wish it would go away. You have even joined Elijah in asking God to take you to heaven so that you can escape sin's disheartening grip. Take courage. God is more powerful than Satan, and He can give you grace to win, one day at a time. If you are now overwhelmed, overcome, and over your head in a besetting sin, seek help. Be honest—the real reason a child of God gives in to temptation is that he chooses to. God will provide a way of victory. You must determine to look for it.

The apostle Paul, who faced constant temptation, wrote, "As it is written, For thy sake we are killed all the day long; we are accounted as sheep for the slaughter. Nay, in all these things we are more than conquerors through him that loved us" (Rom. 8:36–37). What does it mean to be "killed all the day long"? Each temptation offers a choice: surrender to self or die. Through Christ, you can deny self. Like a lamb that willingly faces slaughter, call on Him to show you the way to die. Beg for grace to die to the lust of the moment. Christ, Who endured and conquered all the same temptations you face (Heb. 4:15), lives in you. Victory is yours, one temptation at a time.

Daily Cross-Bearing

In Luke 9:22, Jesus told His disciples He would be rejected, would suffer, and would die on a cross. He said if they wanted to follow Him, they must do the same. "If any man will come after me, let him deny himself, and take up his cross daily, and follow me" (Luke 9:23). How can you do that? Be willing to sacrifice anything God demands to bring glory to Him. This full allegiance has received different names throughout church history—full surrender, consecration, the exchanged life, the Spirit-filled life, and abandonment. It includes a willingness to bear all the "cross-burdens" normal to Christian living, such as ridicule, rejection, satanic attacks, and misunderstood motives.

Whatever you call this cross-bearing, God expects you to do it daily. "Take up your cross daily" means what it says. Each day is new. Today it is time to surrender all to Him. Did you recently ascend the mountaintop of spiritual dedication and abandon all to the will of your Master? So you thought. Today the Holy Spirit reveals a hidden treasure room in your heart, occupied by self. He shows you pride, envy, secret lust, bitterness, or anger toward God. Whatever it is, it must be forsaken today. And it can be! God's mercies arise with each morning sun. He will give you strength this day to conquer sin.

How do you feel at this moment? Do you wish Christ would return because you cannot survive another day? One thing is certain: you can make it through this day. That's all God asks and all He expects. How can you actually do this, rather than just think about it, or just preach it? God's answer is twofold— Begin each day with God, and continue each moment with God.

Begin Each Day with God

I mentioned God's command to pray daily, "Lead us not into temptation" (Matt. 6:13). Each new day begins with the morning. Jesus knows about early morning vulnerability. When you wake up, your mind is empty, open to wrong thinking. Your mind has not yet been girded with His Word. You have heard no music that edifies or conversation that encourages. The moment Satan detects that you are awake, he will begin to sow seeds of sin in your mind. Take offensive action and begin the day with God.

Jeremiah offers words of encouragement about the morning. In the center of Lamentations, the prophet says, "It is of the LORD's mercies that we are not consumed, because his compassions fail not. They are new every morning: great is thy faithfulness" (Lam. 3:22–23). *Mercies* is an all-encompassing Hebrew word found over 250 times in the Old Testament. It describes the goodness of God—His kindness, love, grace, and favor.

Remind yourself every morning that God's mercies are plentiful for each new day. Ask for His mercy as you confess all known sin. Rejoice that you can begin the day with a clean slate. Pray for victory over the evil one. James says, "You have not, because you ask not." Can it be that you do not have victory simply because you fail to ask? Begin the morning by recalling God's mercies. Then ask your heavenly Father to give you courage to run from Satan, to share His cross, and to tackle each challenge of the day.

When I was eight, I discovered on the top shelf of my dad's closet a magic box that he had used to record fascinating images of his World War II navy buddies. It was a Kodak camera, still loaded with a partially used roll of black and white film. I carefully clicked off the rest of the roll and took it to the drug store for developing. When I viewed the results, I was hooked. I knew I could be happy taking pictures for the rest of my life. One year and many rolls later, I saw a TV commercial for the Brownie Starmite camera, which included batteries, film, and a built-in flash. I wanted that camera. Its retail cost was $9.95 plus tax, which would take years to save from my weekly allowance.

On Saturday mornings, I watched a local TV talent show called *Pride of the Southland*. Children of all ages were allowed to showcase their tap dancing, singing, horn blowing, or whatever the station would allow and the public would tolerate. The coveted prize for first place was my dream camera—a Brownie Starmite, which included batteries, film, and a built-in flash.

I mailed in my request to audition for the show. Though I had been taking violin lessons for only a year, I was eager to perform. I watched kids do all kinds of things on the show. If they could perform on television, I thought, so could I. I had nothing to lose. At least I would come home with a lovely parting gift—a package of Kay's Cookies (whoopee). For days I rushed home from school to see if a reply had arrived in the mail. My hero the postman finally delivered, and the postcard said, "Thank you for your request to appear on *Pride of the Southland*. Please report for an audition this Thursday, May 11, at 4 p.m." Yahoo! I was in.

The violin, not an easy instrument for a nine-year-old to play, is almost impossible for a beginner to tune. Noel Gilbert, my patient teacher, would begin each lesson by carefully tuning my instrument for me. I selected a piece, faithfully practiced, and made it through my audition. I was scheduled to appear in June.

On that hot, summer Saturday, I put on my white sport coat, purchased especially for the big day. My parents and teacher stayed home to watch. I was nervous when I got there and shocked when told I would be first on the show.

"Good morning, everyone," said the announcer, "and welcome to *Pride of the Southland*. Our first contestant, a student at East Elementary School, will play on his violin a selection entitled 'The Little Prince.' Let's welcome David Barba." The studio audience clapped politely as I took my place in front of the camera. I lifted my bow carefully and listened as a pianist played the introduction. My big moment had arrived. I mentally pictured myself taking pictures with my new camera, which included batteries, film, and a built-in flash.

Then something happened—that I had not planned. After the first few measures, I knew I had a problem. My finger positions were correct. My bowing was perfect. My bow tie was still on straight. But the sound was horrible. Every time I played a note on the A string, it sounded like a cat with a kidney stone. The notes on the E, D, and G string were fine. But everything on the A string, vitally important for that piece, was flat! Though tempted to run off the stage, I kept sawing away to the miserable end. Certain that I heard a sigh of relief from the studio audience, I slinked over to the announcer, who asked me a few irritating personal questions, gave me a package of Kay's Cookies, and dismissed me to "enjoy" the rest of the program. The judges gave my Brownie Starmite (which included batteries, film, and a built-in flash) to a second-grader in a sequined mini-dress who did something that was supposed to be dancing.

What caused this fiddle fiasco? The answer is obvious. My teacher was not there to tune my instrument. Even if I had remembered to tune it myself, I didn't know how. "The Little Prince" was one sick song because my A string was flat. Though my face turned red on black and white television, the experience was not that bad. During the drive home from my first televised concert, I enjoyed my package of Kay's Cookies. I also relished the attention I got from friends at school who couldn't tell a flat note from a sharp one.

That Saturday morning I learned that no matter how much I had practiced, there was no substitute for a teacher to keep me in tune. Your Teacher is always there to keep you in tune. Seek Him in His Word. Establish contact with Him in prayer. Enjoy His presence.

Continue Each Moment with God

Getting a right start to the day is not difficult, but finishing can be a challenge. Though Satan may retreat and leave you alone for a while, he is always preparing for a fresh attack. Be constantly on guard. Each day is composed of thousands of moments. Work at the holy art of abiding in Christ, staying intimately in touch every moment. If you have idle time, think of Him. When your mind is not occupied, talk to Him. Stay in contact with the King, and you can survive the day.

In His Sermon on the Mount, Jesus gives the key to maintaining contact with Him. First He warns about the sin of worry: "Take no thought for your life, what ye shall eat, or what ye shall drink; nor yet for your body, what ye shall put on" (Matt. 6:25). He then lists five reasons worry is sin. It is needless (6:25), senseless (6:26), useless (6:27), faithless (6:28–30), and godless (6:31–32). Instead of worrying, "Seek ye first the kingdom of God, and his righteousness; and all these things shall be added unto you" (6:33). How can you "seek first" the kingdom of God?

Generally, put God first in every aspect of life. That is, let Him become the lens through which you view everything. Look at all of life through the attributes and characteristics of God. Allow a combination of His character, His attributes, and kingdom principles to become a lighthouse to guide you through decisions, trials, and temptations. To seek first the kingdom of God, meditate on what you know about your King.

What do you know about God?

- He is all-powerful—to supply your power for service (Ps. 63:2).
- He is wisdom—to help you make difficult decisions (Job 12:13; James 1:5).
- He is merciful—to forgive your sin (2 Chron. 30:9).
- He is all grace—to make you what you ought to be (Acts 4:33).
- He is longsuffering—to sympathize with your weakness (Num. 14:18).
- He is all-knowing—to teach you His will (1 Sam. 2:3).
- He is the Comforter—to stay close beside you (John 14:16).

To seek first the kingdom of God, think continuously about Him. Let the Holy Spirit unite your thoughts with the mind of Christ. "Let this mind be in you which was also in Christ Jesus" (Phil. 2:5). He will help you put Him first as you start each day and continue each hour with Him. And as your day comes to a close with joy (and sometimes relief), thank Him for His continuous presence, for His gracious provisions, and for occasionally including film, batteries, and a built-in flash. "Surely goodness and mercy shall follow me all the days [every day] of my life: and I will dwell in the house of the LORD for ever" (Ps. 23:6).

Living Chapter 9

1. Find some biblical illustrations of taking one day at a time.

2. List past personal experiences that were made worse because you did not live them one day at a time. Learn from history.

3. What present conflicts do you face because you are not taking one day at a time? Consider relationships with your spouse, children, and those you serve in ministry.

4. List areas in which you are not willing to take up your cross daily. Surrender each to Him.

5. Pray gratefully: "Father, thank You that all You ask is for me to live this day in Your will. Give me grace to do it."

PRESS *ON!*

. . . FOR THE MINISTRY WIFE

10

You can do anything you ought to do. (Bob Jones Sr.)

For God hath not given us the spirit of fear; but of power, and of love, and of a sound mind. (2 Tim. 1:7)

If you're a pastor's wife, you have a unique job, and not an easy one. It's a job for which you never applied and were never officially hired. Though you have no office, secretary, or salary, some level of production is expected of you. Though you have no written job description, there are strong expectations for your performance (if you don't think so, omit a duty or two and see what happens!), and the roles you're expected to play may not seem to line up with your gifts, dreams, or training. You may have always wanted this job—but more likely, you're surprised to find yourself with the title, and not always happy about it.

But what privileges you have! You aren't spending your life; you're investing it! You are working hand in hand with God's man (and yours), doing what really matters. You are using all your abilities (and some you don't have) building the church Christ loves and died for rather than making yourself or somebody else rich. You won't see your treasures until you get to heaven, but even down here, there are sweet satisfactions in ministry life—if you can manage to avoid a few pitfalls along the road.

The Lord has let me spend my life in ministry—first as a daughter and now as a wife. Though I still have far to go, I've learned much along the way, sometimes through the loving teaching of others and sometimes through the gentle guidance of the Lord Himself. The best lessons, as always, have come through painful experience.

Hoping to help you walk your own ministry road with less pain, more grace, and genuine, deep-down joy, I offer you a few simple lessons I've learned as I've stumbled along my path—lessons I wish I had learned a long time ago.

Stay out of the Prison of Fear

When I conducted a small, unscientific survey of my ministry-wife friends, asking them to name their dominant ministry-related emotion, their overwhelming response was *fear.* I wasn't surprised, for it's mine too. Fear is our common enemy, hindering ministry and making us miserable.

Ministry Fears

Many of our fears are directly related to ministry success. Since all ministry involves risk, some failure is inevitable. Since nobody enjoys that pain, we quickly learn that a sure way to escape it is to avoid risk, sticking steadfastly to the familiar and the comfortable. But the Lord wants His servants to take bold steps of faith with confidence in His faithfulness. "Be strong and of a good courage," He says. "Fear not, nor be afraid . . . for the LORD thy God, he it is that doth go with thee; he will not fail thee, nor forsake thee" (Deut. 31:6).

I am married to a man who loves to test that promise. His favorite form of exercise is jumping off cliffs in great leaps of faith, launching out into the unknown while trusting God alone. Not me. By nature, I'd rather live a beige life and avoid all risk. I prefer to stay safely away from all scary cliffs and behind secure fences and have a quiet picnic as I enjoy the view. When I see my husband considering yet another leap from yet another precipice, it's instinctive for me to try to reason him out of it. But once he's certain of God's will, I know it's my wifely duty to follow. So I close my eyes, hang on tightly to his faith, and take the plunge while inwardly wailing, "I am going to die!"

But I haven't died yet. In fact, every time I've expected to drop into an abyss, I've experienced a gentle glide onto the Solid Rock instead. On the Rock I've enjoyed peace, joy, and blessing (even a picnic or two) and known deep gratitude that I married a man whose faith stretches my own.

The truth is that the fences we think represent security are the walls of the prison of fear instead—fear of the unknown, fear of what others will think, fear of failure. Fear keeps ministry wives, and their husbands with them, in shackles. Fear impedes church planting and thwarts evangelism; it prevents the launch of bold new ministries and paralyzes progress. A fearful spirit is never from the Lord (2 Tim. 1:7).

It's the prison, not the cliff, that's the real scary place. It's dreadful to realize that female anxieties can hinder God's working. When His leading is clear, it's time for you and me to stop digging in our heels and join our husbands in bold strides of faith, not because they are flawless leaders but because it is God's work we are doing, He's the One Who keeps us safe. Remember this: most fear is based not on actual circumstances but on the fear of potential ones. Trust the One Who controls them all and you will find peace. "In the fear of the LORD is strong confidence, and his children shall have a place of refuge" (Prov. 14:26).

Every day, you and your husband stand together on the border of the promised land—the place of God's blessing for those who will just trust Him and jump! His pledge is as true for a wobbly wife as it was for the children of Israel. "Fear not . . . He will not fail thee." Even a cowardly woman on a cliff can be brave while clinging to a promise like that.

Personal Fears

Other ministry-wife fears are much more private, linked to our dread of not measuring up. Some of us genuinely believe ourselves inadequate for ministry responsibilities, but more likely we simply fear being found wanting by others. We worry that if we cannot do and be all people expect, we'll be criticized and rejected. If people reject us, then we can't minister to them—and that would mean failure, since building a ministry requires attracting and keeping people. So, we reason, to be successful in ministry, we must become everything people expect us to be.

If you think this way, you function with fear as your prime motivator, developing such a sensitivity to others' attitudes and comments, such an unhealthy fear of faces (Jer. 1:8, 17), that every ministry gathering will become an emotional risk. You will earnestly but futilely try to please everyone all the time, believing that to be the prerequisite to helping them spiritually. If you let yourself be lured into that trap, you'll soon be the miserable inmate of a dreary prison of fear.

I learned this lesson as a very young pastor's wife. I had a new haircut. My husband liked it and so did I, but I felt nervous as I arrived at the Wednesday prayer service. My hair was dramatically different, and I knew people would notice. One of the first comments came from a middle-aged church leader, a man whose approval I thought I needed. "Nice haircut," he said. "Now you look like a pastor's wife." I recognized the backhanded compliment but resisted the temptation to ask him just what I had looked like before. And actually I was pleased. Hooray for me, I thought. I got it right.

The next Sunday following the morning service, I introduced myself to a visitor. She said, "You're the pastor's wife? I looked all around during the service and didn't see anybody who looked like a pastor's wife." I managed a smile and again withstood the urge to ask her just who or what I looked like. These two people had very different images of some mythical creature named "The Pastor's Wife." Obviously, I couldn't please them both.

As I laughed about it later, I began to understand that people's expectations for me went far beyond haircuts. Each person in the church had a unique job description for me—unwritten and (usually) unspoken expectations for how I should look and what I should do. It was impossible to please them all. I searched the New Testament for God's job description for me. In 1 Timothy 3, I found a list for deacons' wives, but I discovered that the only requirement for a pastor's wife is that there is to be only one of me ("the husband of one wife"). I can handle that! Did the Holy Spirit forget the rest of the list? Did He run out of paper before He got to it? Of course not. The message from this omission is clear. It encourages me, gives me peace, and liberates me from the prison of fear.

God's job description for a ministry wife is this: I am my husband's wife. I am his helpmeet, a helper suited to him. So I go to him and ask "What can I do to help you? What roles can I play that will make your work easier or more effective?" I let him write my job description. He's the perfect one to do it because he knows my skills, my energy level, the needs at home, and my season of life, and he loves me! When I please my husband, I please God, and that gives me confidence.

The way to escape from the prison of fear is not to ignore and disdain what others think and please only yourself. It is to calmly accept that it's normal in ministry to have some rejection and misjudgment, and then just do your best, please your husband, and stay out of the prison of fear.

Remember Who You Are

Who are you? You are not a church employee; you are the servant of the Most High God! Just like Paul, you are "a servant of the Lord Jesus Christ" (Rom. 1:1), called to serve people "for Jesus' sake" (2 Cor. 4:5). You are assigned by Him to a specific place as "a chosen vessel . . . to bear his name" (Acts 9:15). Your commission is from God. You serve Him by serving His people, but they are not your masters. Your ministry is not a plantation with many masters and one slave (you). There is one Master in heaven, and He is the One you are called to please. He is the One you answer to. Do fear displeasing Him, but fear only Him. The people in your ministry are not there to be feared but to be loved and served.

I once had a very ordinary, temporary job. Since it required little skill and few brains, I was well qualified! On the first day, I met my boss, Dan, and after he had explained my duties, I went happily off to work on my own, doing just what he had said to do. Before long, however, things got complicated.

People I didn't recognize began coming by with instructions that were different from those I'd heard from Dan. These well-intentioned folks seemed confident in their authority and certain I would be glad to comply with their instructions, for they were just trying to be helpful. At first I made some adjustments to try to please my self-appointed supervisors, but I quickly realized it was impossible. They contradicted each other, and they contradicted Dan. There was no way to obey my boss and make everybody else happy too.

I became confused and increasingly frustrated. The next time a would-be-boss showed up, I responded to his orders in an assertive voice rare to me, "Sorry. Dan is my boss. I'm going to do exactly what he says and nothing else."

In a huff, that man stomped off—in the direction of Dan's office. I wasn't surprised when at the end of the workday, Dan approached me. “I heard that you said you’re going to do just what I say and nothing else,” he said. I nodded, wondering if it was job-hunting time again. “Good for you,” he continued. “That’s fine with me.” I was relieved—and as pleased as if I had heard him say, “Well done, thou good and faithful servant!” After that day, I relaxed and enjoyed my work, confident that I was pleasing the only one who mattered. I want to hear those extraordinary words of praise from my Master in heaven someday. I know you do too. The only way for us to have that joy is to listen carefully to His voice every moment and then do exactly, and only, what He says. That will please Him.

It may not please everybody else though. People in your ministry, while trying to be helpful, may express desires for you that contradict each other and exceed His expectations. If you struggle to satisfy people—all of them, all the time—your ministry will be motivated not by love and joy but by guilt and dread instead.

Relax. Remember that you have been called and commissioned by God as an instrument to bear His name in a specific place. He Who once willingly made Himself a servant is not a demanding, unreasonable, or capricious Master. His commands are not grievous; His yoke is easy and His burden is light. If at the end of each day, you can stand serenely before your Master, confident that you have followed His instructions, then you are a success. He is pleased with you. You will enjoy a long-term, joyful ministry and can look forward to someday hearing His words: “Well done, thou good and faithful servant!”

Live on the Rock

Our self-existent, never-changing God is the Rock of our strength, the Rock of our salvation. He is our refuge, our high place to hide from the enemy—a solid rock that never crumbles or cracks. A woman who keeps her mind “stayed” on Him will have security, stability, and peace no matter what happens.

> Thou wilt keep him in perfect peace, whose mind is stayed on thee, because he trusteth in thee. Trust ye in the LORD for ever, for in the LORD JEHOVAH is everlasting strength [the Rock of Ages]. (Isa. 26:3–4)

> He is the Rock; his work is perfect: for all his ways are judgment: a God of truth and without iniquity, just and right is he. (Deut. 32:4)

> There is none holy as the LORD: for there is none beside thee: neither is there any rock like our God. (1 Sam. 2:2)

A ministry wife must learn to keep her feet on the Rock because the ministry is by nature a roller-coaster life. There's always something exhilarating or terrifying coming straight at you. But humans need stability—especially female humans. No one can live on a roller coaster. If you tried it, you'd soon be dizzy, nauseated, or dead! Practice living on the Rock instead, keeping your mind settled on truth rather than reacting to your unstable emotions.

Feelings are unreliable. They lie. They register all sorts of exaggerated and imaginary dangers and fail to reflect this spiritual reality: God has a purpose for each of your circumstances. He is working them together for your good as He conforms you to the image of Jesus Christ.

The digital thermometer on our car's dashboard is broken. The poor little thing hasn't been the same since the day in the Mojave Desert when it (accurately) measured 116 degrees. Now it soars and plunges at will, wildly unpredictable and almost never correct. It used to be annoying, but now it's more like a little sideshow keeping me entertained as I drive. I just keep in mind that it doesn't tell the truth. If I need to know an accurate temperature, I tune in to the deep-voiced local radio announcer and trust what he tells me instead.

I'm not bothered too much by this defect in an otherwise reliable car. After all, I have a faulty internal thermometer of my own. It's attached to my emotions—those unreliable feelings that waver wildly, way out of proportion to reality. When a trial brings a bit of heat, my feelings scream that deadly ministry global warming has arrived. Chilly winds of rejection and the icy drizzle of failure instantly freeze my heart in a kind of passive panic. But feelings like those are as untruthful as our car's thermometer, for they don't reflect spiritual reality. Ministry trials by themselves can generate neither dreadful heat nor intolerable cold. The boiling and freezing I sense are simply the faulty reactions of a flawed emotional thermometer to temperate gifts from the hand of the Father.

I can't control how I feel. I'm a human, after all, and a woman besides. But I *can* control how I think. Whenever I marshal my disorderly thoughts and turn them resolutely to truth, my emotions follow. When my mind meditates on promises spoken by the deep, authoritative voice of God, my spirit settles down, steadied by the Word forever settled in heaven. When my mind is stayed on Him, then my heart stops its quivering and is kept in perfect peace. My wild emotional thermometer stabilizes; my heart is "fixed, trusting in the Lord."

Maybe someday we'll get that dashboard thermometer fixed. I can't do it myself, for that job calls for more skill than I have. But with God's help, I can do this: spend less time reacting to my emotions and more time dwelling on truth. Absorbing and understanding truth is a task that requires only the discipline of a daily walk with God. Nothing is more necessary in your daily schedule than sitting at His feet. If God wrote your "to-do" list, He would highlight your time with Him as the highest priority, for He knows that if you want to keep your mind "stayed" on the Rock, you have to keep your nose stuck in the book. "From the end of the earth will I cry unto thee, when my heart is overwhelmed: lead me to the rock that is higher than I" (Ps. 61:2).

I can testify of the joy and satisfaction of the ministry life. I'm sure that you, with me, would say, "This is just a plain old hard job, but we love it!" The ministry stretches faith and strengthens spiritual muscles. It puts calluses on our knees and smiles on our faces. Someday, as you and I stand before the Lord to give account, we'll look back and know our time was well spent. In the meantime, these days serving Him on earth will be more pleasant and productive if we will just stay out of the prison of fear, remember who we are, and live on the Rock.